Green Line

Oberstufe

Abiturthemen 2016
für das erhöhte Niveau

Arbeitsheft Niedersachsen

von
Ilona Aumann
Dr. Peter Bruck
Louise Carleton-Gertsch
Hartmut Klose
Michael Rybicki

Ernst Klett Verlag
Stuttgart · Leipzig

Foreword

Dear Student,

For your final exam in 2016 your curriculum (Kerncurriculum) outlines the topics you have to deal with in the next two years, such as Globalisation, the Individual and Society and Science and Technology.
These topics and the other requirements of the curriculum are covered by your course book **Green Line Oberstufe Niedersachsen**.
In addition there are a number of books and films you need to be familiar with by the time your exam comes round.

This book concentrates on the works on the list for the Abitur 2016: "Billy Elliot", "The Crucible", "My Son the Fanatic", "The Great Gatsby", "Romeo and Juliet" and "The Merchant of Venice".

Your teacher will show you how the study of these works can be integrated into the content of **Green Line Oberstufe Niedersachsen**.
Sometimes texts in the course book will be used to prepare you for themes of the book or film, sometimes the work with this book will replace a section in **Green Line Oberstufe Niedersachsen**.
Many of the exercises and tasks here have references to the Skills section of the course book.
At the end of each chapter your teacher will go back to that part of the course book that develops themes from the work dealt with in the chapter.

Most of the tasks in this workbook are for you to make your own notes and structure your own ideas and thoughts. On the other hand there are many opportunities – some optional – to work with a partner or in a group.
For note taking and structuring your thoughts there is usually space provided in the workbook. For longer written contributions you are usually advised to write these on a separate piece of paper. These pieces of paper can be slipped between the pages of this book so you have everything together. Alternately you could keep them in a separate folder.

The extracts form the two Skakespeare plays are taken form the editions noted on the imprint page. Quotes from *The Crucible* and *The Great Gatsby* refer to the Klett editions of these works (see the imprint page).

The first four chapters in this book are all structured in the same way:

A Introduction
Here you are introduced to the topic or one of the topics of the work, either by referring to a text from your course book or another source.

B Understanding the content
This section gives you space and time to look closely at the work and make sure you understand what happens, for longer works this section is divided into smaller parts so you can make your own notes on the plot and the characters.

C Analysis
The tasks in this part of the chapter enable you to analyse the work, concentrating on characterisation, narrative techniques, language, stylistic devices etc. As with all the tasks in this book there are, where necessary, references to the Skills overview in **Green Line Oberstufe Niedersachsen** to help you. At the end of this book there is a special extra skill about working with films that expands on the skill in your course book.

D Further activities
The final section offers a range of further activities connected with the work. These tasks are mainly designed for partner or group work, continuing the principle of tasks for group or partner work in the other sections in each chapter.

The structure of the Shakespeare chapters is like this:

A Shakespeare for starters
Here is an introduction to the work and to Shakespeare's language.

B Selected extracts and assignments
In this section there are key scenes from the play and tasks to help you understand what is happening and analyse Shakespeare's language and techniques and the characterisation of the protagonists. There are also many tasks for group work.

C More on the play
The last section contains mediation and listening comprehension tasks.

Enjoy working with this workbook and good luck with your exam preparations.

Your Green Line Oberstufe Niedersachsen Team

Symbols

[👥]	Do this task with another person.
[👥👥]	Do this task in a (small) group.
→S24	This is a reference to the Skills section of *Green Line Oberstufe Niedersachsen* (ISBN 978-3-12-594006-2) or to the book *Essential skills* (ISBN 978-3-12-601041-2)

Contents

Chapter 1   Billy Elliot

A Introduction 4

B Understanding the content 5

C Analysis 12

D Further activities 16

Chapter 2   The Crucible

A Introduction 20

B Understanding the content 21

C Analysis 31

D Further activities 41

Chapter 3   My Son the Fanatic*

A Introduction 44

B Understanding the content 48

C Analysis 55

D Further activities 59

Chapter 4   The Great Gatsby

A Introduction 62

B Understanding the content 63

C Analysis 68

D Further activities 75

Chapter 5   Romeo and Juliet**

A Shakespeare for starters 80

B Selected extracts and assignments 82

C More on the play 108

Chapter 6   The Merchant of Venice**

A Shakespeare for starters 110

B Selected extracts and assignments 112

C More on the play 135

* contains the complete short story
** contains extracts from the play

Chapter 1 *Billy Elliot*

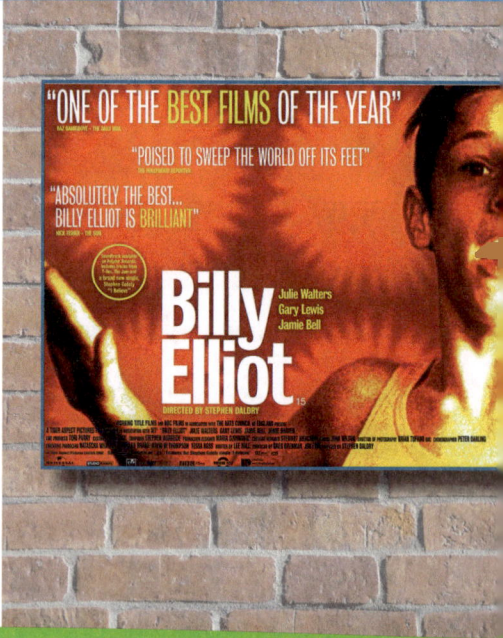

A Introduction

1 **Discussion:** Read the text "Boys like bashing drums and girls prefer the flute. So what?" on page 90 in *Green Line Oberstufe Niedersachsen*.
Discuss to what extent the text reflects typical gender issues. → S26

2 **Viewing:** Watch the trailer of the movie twice. Speculate on what the film is going to be about. Use the following grid for your notes.

> **TIP**
>
> Sometimes you may find it difficult to understand the dialect from the Northeast of England. Select the option with English subtitles to help you.

Setting	Characters	Special incidents	Further details	Music
boxing club – boxing ring				
ballet class – ballet exercises				
private home				
coal fields				
pit village – terraced houses, working class settlement				

Billy Elliot | 1

coastal site					
protests, demonstrations					

3 *Jot down your assumptions in about five sentences.*

_____
_____
_____
_____
_____
_____
_____

B Understanding the content

1 [👥] *Watch the film at least once. Find the correct chronological order and compare your results with your partner.*

- ☐ Billy is invited to join Mrs Wilkinsons's dancing class.
- ☐ Jackie and Tony take him to the express bus to London.
- ☐ Billy has to go to boxing practice because it's a family tradition – both his father and grandfather were enthusiastic boxers.
- ☐ Billy prepares breakfast for himself and his senile grandmother every morning as his mother died several years earlier.
- ☐ When Jackie and Tony find out Billy has been going to dancing classes there is a big row.
- ☐ Jackie is finally convinced his son has a talent for dancing.
- ☐ His family do not know that he has become interested in dancing.
- ☐ So Jackie goes with Billy to London for the audition.
- ☐ Billy is not really good at boxing.
- ☐ When Jackie comes across Billy and Michael in the gym on Christmas Eve, Billy reacts with a defiant, passionate dance.
- ☐ Billy gets a place at the Royal Ballet School.
- ☐ Billy fights to realise his dream and Mrs Wilkinson gives him free tuition to prepare for the audition at the Royal Ballet School.
- ☐ After a long time a letter arrives in Durham.
- ☐ Jackie even becomes a strike breaker to earn money to support Billy in London.
- ☐ Some years later Tony and Jackie go to London to see Billy in his first starring role in *Swan Lake*.

TIP

Your teacher will give you a list of words and phrases to help you unterstand the film.

1 Billy Elliot

2 *Explain the following chapter titles.*

> **Dad's Decision**
>
> **A Ghost Story** (Plot of Swan Lake)
>
> **The Audition**
>
> **A Disgrace to the Gloves**
>
> **Tony's Arrest**

3 *Reading:* Read the following two summaries and underline helpful phrases and expressions. →S13

> **TIP**
>
> Writing a summary is a good way to prove that you have understood the main aspects and motifs of the movie.

> **TIP**
>
> This summary was written by native speakers of English for a movie website. The language should be all right, but what about the content?

Summary 1

The film's setting is a small pit village in Durham during the miners' strike in the mid 80s. At the centre of the film is the Elliot family – 11-year-old Billy (newcomer Jamie Bell), his elder brother Tony (Jamie Draven), their widowed father Jackie (Gary Lewis) and Nan (Jean Heywood), the boys' confused grandmother. Jackie and Tony are both
5 coal miners out on strike.

Male members of the Elliot family traditionally work down the pit and box in their spare time. Jackie enrolls Billy for boxing instruction at the Sports Centre, but Billy does not take it up with much enthusiasm and it is plain that his heart isn't in it. Because the basement of the Centre is being used a soup kitchen for the striking
10 miners, the ballet classes usually held there have to share the hall with the boxers. Thus Billy finds an alternative to boxing. He joins the ballet class and discovers his passion for dancing. When Jackie finds out and places a ban on ballet, Billy continues to take lessons secretly with his teacher Sandra Wilkinson (Julie Walters).

Mrs Wilkinson believes Billy has the talent to gain a place at the Royal Ballet School.
15 She arranges an audition, but on the day before Tony is arrested during a strikers' protest and Billy misses the audition. Mrs Wilkinson tries to convince Jackie that Billy should grasp the chance of becoming a professional ballet dancer, but Jackie and Tony are appalled at the idea, since ballet is only something for "poofs".

Christmas is hard for the Elliot family. However, Billy has not given up on his dream
20 and finds support from his best friend, Michael (Stuart Wells), who comes out as gay.

By chance, Jackie comes across Billy dancing in the gym and realises that his son has talent. This convinces him that he has
25 to support his son whatever it takes, even if it means crossing the picket line to earn the money for Billy's training. Tony manages to stop his father from becoming
30 a "scab" and instead the whole community gets involved in raising money for Billy.

Jackie accompanies Billy on the trip to London for the audition at the Royal Ballet School. Although he performs well, Billy is so nervous that he attacks another boy in the changing rooms, for which he is severely reprimanded by the panel of judges. The audition seems doomed until in a final question Billy is asked what it feels like when he's dancing. His reply is "like electricity". After what seems like an eternity, Billy receives a letter of acceptance from the School and leaves for London.

Fourteen years later in the late 90s Jackie and Tony attend the premiere of a modern interpretation of "Swan Lake" in London with Billy (dancer/actor Adam Cooper) in the lead role. Also in the audience is Michael.

Billy Elliot 1

Summary 2

Billy Elliot is 11 years old. He lives in a mining village in the North. His mother has died some years ago. He lives with his father Jackie and his brother Tony and his demented grandmother.

Billy should learn boxing like his father and grandfather because that is tradition
5 in the family. But Billy isn't good at boxing and he sees some girls dancing at the gym. He likes it better than boxing and starts to dance with the girls at the gym. His father and anybody else must not know it and he conceals it from them. But Mrs Wilkinson, who is the dancing teacher, knows his talent and assists him with his dream. Then Jackie and Tony find out about the ballet training and there is a big conflict.
10 Jackie thinks Billy will become a "poof". Secretly Billy fights for his dream and Mrs Wilkinson gives him free dancing classes because he has an audition with the Royal Ballet School in London.

One day at Christmas Billy is dancing with his best friend Michael in the gym and his father sees him and so Billy dances as never before in great anger and defiance
15 and with great passion. His father has now a different opinion and thinks Billy is good. He even becomes a strikebreaker to get the money for Billy. Then he goes to London for the audition, but nervous Billy hits a boy in the changing rooms, even though he has done well at dancing and answered a question well.

Then Billy and his father go home and wait a long time for a letter. Then it comes
20 and Billy is admitted. So, with his father and his brother, he goes to catch the bus to London.

Several years later Billy takes the lead in "Schwanensee" in London and Jackie and Tony are in the audience and are very proud of Billy Elliot.

> **TIP**
>
> This summary was written by a German school student. Here you need to look at both the language and the content.

4 *Compare the two summaries and decide which one you like better for what reason.*

5 *Improve the summary of your choice by adding facts or deleting some aspects.*

6 *Writing: Now write a condensed and simplified version of about 50 words on an extra sheet of paper.*

Detailed viewing

At the beginning of this section you will get a card with an item (word/motif) on it which plays a specific role in the movie. Pay special attention to this item when watching the movie again. There will be a task on this item later (Analysis C, task 7).

7 [👥] *After you have watched "Billy Elliot" once, read through the following statements. Then, while watching the chapters (1–4 up to 22:03) of the movie again, put the letter of the correct answer into the box below. In each case, only **one** answer is correct. Check your results with a partner.*

1. At the beginning of the movie Billy is about
   a) 15 years old.
   b) 11 years old.
   c) 8 years old.

2. Billy lives together with his
   a) old granny.
   b) father, mother and his brother Tony.
   c) widowed father, Tony and his old granny.

3. In his village Everington there are protests going on because
   a) the workers are fighting for better working conditions.
   b) the workers are fighting against the government's plans to close down pits.
   c) workers feel steel production should be increased.

4. Billy is crazy about
   a) boxing.
   b) wrestling.
   c) playing his mum's piano.

1 Billy Elliot

5. Billy becomes slowly interested in
   a) a group of ballet dancers next to the boxing ring.
   b) one of the girls in the ballet group.
   c) training intensively for boxing competitions.

6. In the mobile library Billy
   a) steals a book on ballet.
   b) gives back a book about dementia.
   c) borrows a book on Fred Astaire.

7. Billy starts practising ballet regularly
   a) with his best friend Michael.
   b) with the group of his ballet teacher's daughter.
   c) at home and in ballet classes.

8. The workers show
   a) strong disapproval of strike breakers.
   b) encouragement for people crossing picket lines.
   c) sympathy for the police force.

1. ☐ 2. ☐ 3. ☐ 4. ☐ 5. ☐ 6. ☐ 7. ☐ 8. ☐

8 *Now complete the following tasks in your own words on a separate piece of paper.*

1. Write down your impressions of Billy's home in the first 20 minutes of the film.
2. Describe Billy's feelings during the boxing session at the club / gym.
3. Why does Billy feel attracted to the ballet classes?
4. Describe Billy's relationship with his family.
5. Note down the most striking things you notice about Billy's home.
6. How does Michael feel about what Billy is doing?

9 *Watch the next chapters (5–8) of the movie (22:04 up to 52:05).*
Complete the following sentences. Then compare your completed sentences in a small group with other students.

1. Jackie, Billy's father, is puzzled and embarrassed about Billy's absence at the boxing club because _____

2. At the supermarket Jackie and Tony are upset because _____

3. Jackie is very mad and disappointed about Billy because _____

4. At the Wilkinson's house Billy is confronted with _____

5. Mrs Wilkinson offers Billy individual training sessions because _____

Billy Elliot | 1

6. Michael dresses up in women's clothes and _____
   _____
   _____
   _____

7. The first individual dancing lesson is a special one because _____
   _____
   _____
   _____

8. Tony and his father Jackie get into a big fight because _____
   _____
   _____
   _____

9. Billy and Mrs Wilkinson argue about the following points: _____
   _____
   _____
   _____

10. On the ferry Billy learns about "Swan Lake", which contains the following details: _____
    _____
    _____
    _____

10 *Watch the next chapters (9–11) of the movie (52:06 up to 01:04:47). Decide whether the following statements are true or false. If necessary, correct the statement.*

	True	False	Correction
1. The police think that Tony is one of the leaders of the strike.			
2. Tony is able to escape from the police.			
3. Billy does not cancel the audition with Mrs Wilkinson.			
4. During the fierce discussion at Billy's house he does not start dancing because he is very insecure.			
5. Mrs Wilkinson pays a visit to the Elliot family to clarify the situation around Billy's application.			

1 | Billy Elliot

	True	False	Correction
6. Michael believes in Billy and supports him at all times.			
7. On Christmas Day the Elliot family happily celebrates Christmas together.			
8. Jackie chops up Billy's mother's piano.			
9. Michael openly shows his orientation and feelings for Billy.			
10. Billy returns Michael's affection.			

11 *Match the parts of the sentences according to what happens in the next chapters (12 – 13) of the movie (1:04:48 to 1:17:13). Then put them in the correct order. Put your answers in the boxes below.*

1. Billy starts dancing in front of his father
2. Jackie goes to a broker's
3. Michael and Billy talk about French ballet expressions
4. Since Jackie does not react directly
5. This information shows Jackie
6. Jackie even goes back to work and thus becomes a "scab" himself
7. When Jackie enters the gym
8. Jackie visits the Wilkinsons' house
9. Even Tony supports his brother
10. This performance convinces Jackie

a) Michael feels embarrassed at wearing a tutu.
b) in order to find about how much a career in ballet would cost.
c) that Billy is a truly gifted dancer.
d) though he does not betray the miners' ideals and pride.
e) though he knows this would betray the miners' cause.
f) since Michael is interested in everything to do with ballet.
g) that he has to so everything to support his younger son.
h) because he feels the strength and motivation to show him how good he really is.
i) Billy is very disappointed.
j) in order to get some more money for his dead wife's jewellery.

1. ☐ 2. ☐ 3. ☐ 4. ☐ 5. ☐ 6. ☐ 7. ☐ 8. ☐ 9. ☐ 10. ☐

Billy Elliot | 1

12 Watch the next chapters (14 – 16; 1:17:13 – 1:37:45). Answer the following tasks in your own words. Fill in the cards and compare your results with your neighbour.

1. In the changing room what does the other boy want to know and what is revealed through the scene?

2. What does Jackie experience during Billy's application procedure?

3. How does the audition itself go?

4. What happens after the audition in the changing room?

5. Explain how Billy and his family react when the letter arrives.

6. Describe Billy's farewell to Everington.

1 Billy Elliot

13 [👥] *Before watching the last chapter (17) of "Billy Elliot" (1:37:46 up to the closing credits) read through the following. Then, while watching, tick the correct answers. In each case, only **one** answer is correct. Exchange your findings with a partner.*

1. The last scene of the movie takes place about
   a) a couple of months later.
   b) 5 years later.
   c) 14 years later.

2. Tony and Jackie are attending a ballet at Covent Garden and
   a) are right on time.
   b) miss the first half of the piece.
   c) miss just a couple of minutes.

3. Billy is informed via a member of staff that
   a) some members of his family are there.
   b) Tony, Jackie, Michael and a male friend are there.
   c) Tony, Jackie and Michael are there.

4. It is a performance of
   a) a modern tap dance production.
   b) a version of Swan Lake.
   c) a free dance production.

5. Billy
   a) plays a minor character in that production.
   b) has the leading role in that production.
   c) is the producer behind the stage production.

6. During the performance
   a) Jackie is deeply touched.
   b) Jackie bursts into tears.
   c) Jackie is extremely proud of Billy.

1. ☐   2. ☐   3. ☐   4. ☐   5. ☐   6. ☐

C Analysis

1 [👥👥] *Look at the following list of typical motifs found in film and literature. Referring to "Billy Elliot" make a list of the five motifs that are most central to the film. In a small group agree on three motifs.*

friendship	maleness	courage	insecurity
family	love	progress	growing up
change	planning life	choices	aggression
trust	individuality	education	prejudice
class	journey	dreams	distance
wealth versus poverty	trust	rural versus urban	fear

2 *Look at these screen shots from the film.*

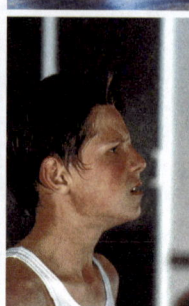

Billy Elliot 1

a) *Choose four that show Billy's development as a dancer. Describe the kind of shot each one is and what you can see in it.* →S28

b) *Choose the two shots that show conflicts. Say what part of the film the shot was taken from and what happens before and after. Describe how the shot shows the conflict between the people you can see in it.*

TIP

For this task refer to the special skill on the visual aspects of film that your teacher will give you.

3 *Write a sentence the following people might have said about Billy's passion for dancing. Sometimes they might have said different things at different times during the film.*

Mrs Wilkinson: _____

_____

Billy's father Jackie: _____

_____

Michael: _____

_____

Tony: _____

_____

4 *Vocabulary: Talking about characters.*
Look at this list of words to characterise people. Look up words you are not sure about in your dictionary.

a_ active	e_ easy-going	likeable	resolute
afraid	efficient	lonely	responsible
ambitious	embarrassed	loyal	romantic
ambiguous	energetic	m_ manipulative	ruthless
anxious	envious	mature	s_ self-assured
apprehensive	f_ faithful	miserable	self-confident
ashamed	fearful	moral	sensitive
b_ brave	fragile	n_ naïve	sensible
c_ caring	frustrated	nervous	strong-willed
charming	furious	o_ obsessed with	successful
cheerful	g_ goal-oriented	optimistic	sure of oneself
cold-blooded	h_ happy	p_ passionate	t_ tender
confident	hopeful	pessimistic	tense
controlling	hurt	positive	triumphant
cruel	i_ impatient	proud	troubled
d_ dedicated	5,3 mm	provocative	u_ unbalanced
desperate		r_ racist	unkind
destructive		radiant	v_ vulnerable
determined	j_ jealous	rational	w_ weak
dissatisfied	joyful	rebellious	wild
dominating	l_ lawless	remorseless	worried

a) *Work on your own. Tick the ones that match Billy.*
b) [👥] *With a partner compare your results and defend your choices with examples from the movie.* →S24, →S26
c) *Which words from the list describe best the way you see Jackie?*

1 | Billy Elliot

5 *Did your attitude towards or opinion about Billy change throughout the movie? Explain why.*

6 [👥] *You are a member of the Royal Ballet School admissions board. Complete the form by ticking Billy's answers to the questions. Add some more questions in the space below and tick the answers Billy would have given.*
Compare your results with your partner and agree on the answers Billy would have given.

| A – absolutely   B – yes   C – not sure   D – no   E – absolutely not |

	A	B	C	D	E
1. Do you like wrestling?					
2. Are you comfortable meeting new people?					
3. Do you enjoy spending a lot of time by yourself?					
4. Are you often frustrated?					
5. Are you often in a good mood?					
6. Can God influence your life?					
7. Do you enjoy life?					
8. Is your family supportive?					
9. Do you like your neighbourhood?					
10. Can you enjoy life without worrying to much about your future?					
11. Do you have many close friends?					
12. Do you believe you are much stronger than it appears?					
13. Do you worry about what other people might think about you?					
14. Do you like nature?					
15. Are you ambitious?					
16. Would you say that people need gumption to get through life?					
17. Are you afraid of anything new?					
18. Are you able to struggle no matter what life throws at you?					
19.					
20.					

7 a) [👥] *Before watching the movie each of you were given a card with a central motif/word on it. Get together with a classmate who has the same motif/key word and decide what this word/item stands for.*

Example: The golden wedding ring of Billy's dead mother is the most precious memory Jackie has got. The fact that he takes this ring to a broker shows how much he is willing to give for his son Billy.

_____
_____
_____
_____
_____

b) *Make a poster with all of the results.*

Billy Elliot | 1

8 *The following excerpt from the movie (0:22:25 – 0:28:15) takes place after the main character Billy has found out about his passion for ballet. After experiencing that ballet is hard work that requires a lot of rehearsing and practising Billy finally has a feeling of success, which makes him feel proud and self-confident. He has found something he can fully identify with.*
Analyse the excerpt with regard to cinematic devices and narrative technique. Focus on montage, camera operations, visual symbols and special emphasis, e.g. through music. The key words might help you to organise your results. →S29

TIP
For this task refer to the special skill on the visual aspects of film that your teacher will give you.

Narrative techniques

appearance of main characters involved

Billy: _____

Jackie: _____

Nanny: _____

body language

Billy: _____

Jackie: _____

use of language

_____

setting

_____

plot

_____

suspense

_____

Cinematic devices

camera operations

_____

other effects

_____

visual symbols

_____

film music / sound

_____

Main function of the exerpt

_____

D Further activities

1 Mediation: *Read the following articles. Decide which one you are going to tell your class about.* →S33
a) *Tell your class about what happened during the strike and the situation in the British coal industry today.*

Großbritannien: 20 Jahre nach dem einjährigen Bergarbeiterstreik

Zwanzig Jahre nach dem Bergarbeiterstreik, der die Hintergrundgeschichte für den Roman „Billy Elliot" darstellt, griffen viele Zeitungen den historischen Streik noch einmal auf. Die Bergleute reagierten mit ihrem Streik auf die gesamtwirtschaftliche Krise, die ihre Existenzen im traditionellen Kohleabbau bedrohte. Der Streik hatte vom 20.03.1984 bis zum 03.03.1985 fast ein Jahr lang gedauert.

Für die Bergarbeiter selbst waren die Folgen des Streiks verheerend. Als der Streik begann, gab es in GB noch 170 Zechen, in denen über 181 000 Menschen beschäftigt waren und 90 Millionen Tonnen Kohle produziert wurden. Heute gibt es noch 15 Zechen, in denen etwa 6500 Menschen arbeiten. Etwa 3000 weitere arbeiten im Tagebau. Einstige klassische Bergbaugebiete wie Durham und Lancashire haben heute keine Zechen mehr. Die Nationale Gewerkschaft (NUM) ist auf einen Rumpf mit wenigen tausend Mitgliedern reduziert worden, die in dem Industriezweig arbeiten.

Die Leiden der Bergarbeiter während des Streiks waren fast ohne Beispiel. Etwa 20 000 Bergarbeiter wurden verletzt und mussten zum Teil im Krankenhaus behandelt werden, 13000 wurden festgenommen, 200 ins Gefängnis gesteckt, zwei wurden beim Streikpostenstehen getötet, drei starben im Winter beim Kohlesammeln und 966 wurden entlassen.

Die Bergarbeiter sahen sich brutalen Angriffen der Polisei ausgesetzt, die zu Unterdrückungsmethoden griff, wie sie auf der britischen Insel bis dahin unbekannt gewesen waren. Berittene Polizisten griffen Streikposten an und verbreiteten in Bergarbeitersiedlungen Angst und Schrecken. Eine neu gebildete, nationale Kampftruppe aus schwer bewaffneten Polizisten führte militärische Attacken gegen die Bergleute. Die Bergarbeiter wurden daran gehindert, sich frei im Land zu bewegen, uns es wurden Sondergerichte gebildet, um mit der großen Zahl Festgenommener fertig zu werden.

Die NUM wurde gerichtlich angegriffen, und es gab mehrere Versuche, ihr Vermögen zu beschlagnahmen. Mächtige Wirtschaftsinteressen und der Staatsapparat organisierten gemeinsam eine massive Streikbrecheroperation, die in der Gründung einer Streikbrecherorganisation gipfelte, der „Gewerkschaft demokratischer Bergarbeiter".

Nach der Niederlage des Streiks kam es noch schlimmer. Zechenschließungen zogen den Abstieg ganzer Kommunen in verzweifelte Armut nach sich. Viele Jugendliche mussten ihre Heimat verlassen, und in jeder dritten zurückgebliebenen Familie stellten sich, wie eine Studie feststellte, ernste Suchprobleme ein.

Chris Marsden und Julie Hyland *wsws.org*,
6. April 2004

b) **Describe** the way Jamie Bell's life developed after the success of "Billy Elliot".

Billy Elliot – „Ballett ist doch was für Mädchen"

Jamie Bell (14), Bergarbeitersohn aus Nordengland, spielt als „Billy Elliot" die Rolle seines Lebens. *Von Nina Rehfeld*

Berühmt, findet Jamie Bell, ist man, „wenn man auf einem Balkon steht und einem die Menge zujubelt. Ist mir bisher nicht passiert." Jamie Bell ist 14 Jahre alt und auf bestem Weg, berühmt zu werden - als Berg-
5 arbeitersohn, der unbedingt Tänzer werden will, in Stephen Daldrys Geniestreich „Billy Elliot". Eine Nominierung als Bester Europäischer Darsteller hat dem Jungen aus dem nordenglischen Billingham die Rolle schon eingebracht, nicht wenige Kritiker sprechen von
10 einem Oscar-reifen Auftritt.

Seit er fünf ist, nimmt Jamie Bell Tanzunterricht. Ein begnadeter Tänzer ist der Teenager, der das gefällige Boygroup-Gehopse seiner Altersgenossen als „nichtssagenden Mist" verachtet, nicht. Ein wenig zu steif die
15 Arme, ein bisschen zu hölzern seine Schritte. Doch genau Bells kantige Körperlichkeit und die unbändige Wut, die sich darin bricht, machen „Billy Elliot" zum Erlebnis.

Jamie selbst ist von dem Rummel um ihn eher über-
20 rascht. Ein typischer Halbwüchsiger, der mit gesenktem Blick und schüchternem Grinsen die Schmeicheleien des großen Medieninteresses mehr erduldet als genießt. „Man kann durch meine Augen in Billys Seele sehen?", gibt er staunend eine Reporterfrage zurück.
25 „Na ja, vielleicht mit Röntgenblick." Wahrscheinlich kennt er das, was Billy Elliot im Film durchmacht, selbst zu gut, als dass er sich seine Darstellung als außerordentliche Leistung ankreiden könnte.

Wie Billy entschloss sich auch Jamie einst unter dem
30 Gelächter seiner Freunde, zum Ballettunterricht zu gehen - statt mit den Kumpels auf dem Fußballplatz zu bolzen. Ebenso wie Billy hörte er sich an: „Balletttanzen ist doch was für Mädchen!" Und wie Billy bestärkte das den eigensinnigen Jungen, der mit seiner Mutter
35 und seiner fünf Jahre älteren Schwester aufwuchs, nur noch. „Ich wollte ihnen zeigen, dass Tanzen eben nicht bloß für Mädchen ist", sagt Jamie.

Über 2000 Jungs casteten Regisseur Stephen Daldry und Produzent John Finn. Drei Mal hatten sie Jamie
40 bereits gesehen, als er es endlich in die Endauswahl schaffte. Jetzt türmen sich die Filmangebote für den sommersprossigen Briten mit den abstehenden Ohren, die so wunderbar erröten, wenn er wütend wird. Gerade hat er fürs britische Fernsehen eine Serie ab-
45 gedreht, im kommenden Jahr will er einen zweiten Kinofilm mit dem Titel „Suedehead" machen. Es geht um einen Jungen, der zwischen die Fronten einer schwarzen und einer Skinhead-Gang gerät. Trotzdem will er erst die mittlere Reife machen, bevor er sich ganz fürs Filmbiz entscheidet - auch wenn die Schule 50 ihm „schrecklich langweilig" erschien, als er nach den Dreharbeiten zurückkehrte. „Für den Fall, dass ich als Schauspieler auf die Klappe falle."

Erste Bekanntschaft mit der Unbill des Starrummels hat Jamie bereits gemacht. Bei der Premiere von Jim 55 Carreys Weihnachtsmärchen „The Grinch" in London erreichte ihn die Nachricht, dass Popsternchen Britney Spears nach einem Auftritt in einem nahen Restaurant weilte und ihn gerne kennen lernen würde. „Ich habe mich erst mal auf dem Klo eingeschlossen, 60 meine besten Kumpel angerufen und gekreischt: Was mach ich nur? Was mach ich nur?", gesteht Jamie. „Ich wäre fast explodiert!"

Natürlich fuhr er hin, nur um festzustellen, dass noch 50 andere Vips dort darauf warteten, Britney die Hand 65 zu schütteln. Drei Stunden wartete die Meute, bis Britney mitteilen ließ, sie habe nun doch keine Lust mehr. „Die Ziege!", entfährt es Jamie Bell, und seine Ohren leuchten feuerrot. „Eine totale Zeitverschwendung. Traue nie einem Popstar!" 70

Bleibt die Frage nach Jamies Zukunftsplänen. „Die Schule fertig machen, ein paar gute Filme drehen und eine gewisse Künstlerin kennen lernen", grinst er. Trotzdem er so schmählich sitzen gelassen wurde? „Natürlich!", bricht es aus ihm heraus. „Sie hat mir das 75 Herz gebrochen, und ich fühle mich schrecklich, das zu sagen!" Vielleicht also doch ein Glück, dass Jamie auf dem Weg zum Filmstar ist. „Könnte sein", überlegt er, „dass ich sie demnächst auf irgendeiner Vip-Party treffe." 80

Die Welt, 30.11.2000

Billy Elliot

2 After the great success of the movie in the year 2000 Melvin Burgess turned Lee Hall's film script into a novel in 2001. At the same time plans were made to turn the story into a musical, which successfully premiered in London's West End and on Broadway in New York in 2005. The music for the lyrics, again by Lee Hall, was composed by Sir Elton John.

One of the crucial scenes in the sequence at the audition board is when Billy is asked what it feels like when he dances. Here are two excerpts from the novel and a song from the musical that refer to this scene.

a) **Listening:** Listen to the song "Electricity" and fill in the gaps on the worksheet your teacher will give you.

b) **Reading:** Read the two excerpts from the novel by Melvin Burgess. In this novel the story of Billy is told from different angles / perspectives (e.g. from Billy's, Tony's, Jackie's … perspective). Here you find Billy's and Jackie's perspective on the audition at the Royal Ballet School towards the end of the novel. Compare the different points of view.

> **Billy Elliot:**
> And that was about it. Complete f***ing disaster. The last thing they asked was what it felt like when I was dancing. What was the point? They come from a different planet than people like me and me dad. And anyhow, how can you say something about that – that feeling you get when you forget where you are and what you're
> 5 doing and even why you're doing it? It just is, that's all.
> Then we went home.
>
> From: Melvin Burgess, *Billy Elliot*, The Chicken House, 2001

> **Jackie Elliot:**
> And right at the end of the audition, Billy had said this thing. We were almost on our way out when one of them asked him what it felt like when he danced and Billy … well, he's like me, not so good with words, but even so. I really think what he said had an effect.
> 5 He said, "Dunno" – which was what he'd said to every other bloody question they'd asked him. But then he had a little think and he said something about it feeling like flying.
> "It starts off sort of stiff," he said, "but once I get going I forget what's going on and I sort of disappear. Like there's fire in me whole body. Like a bird. Like
> 10 electricity," he said. "Yeah. Like electricity."
> I saw the people on the panel glance at one another and I felt a little tingle go down my spine then, because I knew he'd impressed them. He'd impressed me anyhow. Maybe they weren't as bad as they looked …When we left one of them wished me good luck with the strike, so he must have been on our side.
>
> From: Melvin Burgess, *Billy Elliot*, The Chicken House, 2001

> **TIP**
>
> "Milling around" is an activity in which the whole class moves around the classroom and each student contacts other students in order to talk to them and exchange ideas.

c) **Discussion:** Which version of the scene do you like best (film, musical, novel)? Mill around in class and exchange arguments with various people. →S24

3 Go to the opening pages of the Topic "The individual and society" in *Green Line Oberstufe Niedersachsen* (pages 68/69)

a) Study Abraham Maslow's "Hierachy of Needs" Then comment on this pyramid in terms of Billy's personal situation and development throughout the movie.

b) On these pages there are six quotations about the individual and society. Choose the two that have the most relevance for Billy and comment on them in terms of Billy's personality.

Billy Elliot | 1

4 [👥] ***Creative writing:*** Get together in teams of three or four and write the script for a scene between Billy and one or more people from Everington. This is the background to the scene:

> After Billy's first year at the Royal Ballet School in London he returns to Everington to spend his holidays there. He meets Michael, Mrs Wilkinson, and of course he is happy to be with his brother Tony and his father Jackie again. In the meantime his nanny has died. He is sad about it and is reminded of his mum's death.

*Before you start, look at the screenplay of "The Queen and the PM" on pages 18/19 in **Green Line Oberstufe Niedersachsen**. This will give you an idea of what a screenplay looks like.*
Your script should include the following points:

- where the meeting takes place
- questions to Billy about life at the Royal Ballet School and his replies
- questions from Billy to the other person(s)
- information about life in Everington since Billy has been away
- how Billy and the other person(s) react to what is said
- the future

In addition you could add information about the camera work. →S29

TIP

Make sure to use the correct register and vocabulary for your dialogues. It is helpful to remember the personalities of the characters.

5 [👥] ***Role play:*** After Billy's audition in London the members of the board meet to decide on whether to offer Billy a place at the Royal Ballet School.
Work in groups of four and choose one of the following roles:

1. You are convinced Billy is just right for the School.
2. You think it would be a mistake to offer Billy a place.
3. You see Billy's undoubted talent but are not sure about his background.
4. You are worried about his violent streak and lack of articulation.

Act out the discussion. You know the board decides to offer Billy a place, so you have to reach a decision and make compromises. →S26

TIP

When you have chosen a role, work on the details of your position. Look at the scene with the audition again and take into consideration what else you know of Billy and his background. Don't forget the results of the questionnaire (C6)!

Chapter 2 *The Crucible*

A Introduction

1 [👥] ***Discussion:*** *Read the following quotations as well as those on pages 68 to 69 in* Green Line Oberstufe Niedersachsen. *Choose the one that you like the most, and think about the reason for your choice. Then discuss your ideas with a partner.* →S26

to overwhelm *überwältigen*
to own oneself to be in control of one's own life

to be equally true to be also true
law enforcement *Gesetzesvollzug*

to menace to threaten
perpetually continuously
disintegration *Zerfall*
primary basic
hostility the feeling that someone is your enemy

> The individual has always had to struggle to keep from being overwhelmed by the tribe. If you try it, you will be lonely often, and sometimes frightened. But no price is too high to pay for the privilege of owning yourself.
> Rudyard Kipling
>
> Every society gets the kind of criminal it deserves. What is equally true is that every community gets the kind of law enforcement it insists on.
> Robert F. Kennedy
>
> Civilized society is perpetually menaced with disintegration through this primary hostility of men towards one another.
> Sigmund Freud
>
> A nation's greatness is measured by how it treats its weakest members.
> Mahatma Ghandi

2 a) *Brainstorm:* *What associations does the expression "witch-hunt" bring to your mind? Note down your thoughts.*

b) ***Brainstorm:*** *In class brainstorm historical examples of witch-hunts you have heard or read about.*

The Crucible | 2

B Understanding the content

1 *As you read the play, fill in the fact sheet on "The Crucible".*

Author:	
Genre:	
Year of publication:	
Setting (time and place):	
Type of narrator:	
Role of narrator:	
Protagonist:	
Characters – girls:	
Characters – villagers:	
Characters – figures of authority:	
Main themes:	

2 a) [👥] *Below is a description of 19 of the 21 characters, as well as a quotation from the play describing them. As you read the play, try to work out who is who and add the names of the characters to the list. You will need some time to complete the list, as not everyone appears in Act One. Afterwards, compare your notes with those of a partner.* →S11
  b) *You will find that two of the characters in the list are not described in the stage directions or by the narrator, one of whom plays a major role in the play. Discuss with a partner why you think this might be.* →S26

> **TIP**
>
> **The descriptions.** When the characters enter, they are often either described in the stage directions or (in Act One) by the narrator.

Character	Quotation	Description
1.	*there is very little good to be said for him; he believed he was being persecuted wherever he went; a widower with no interest in children, or talent with them*	Minister in Salem; tries to strengthen his position through the witch trials
2.	*nearing forty, a tight-skinned, eager-eyed intellectual*	Minister in Beverly; invited to Salem to see if witchcraft is at work; supports the witch trials but later denounces them
3.	*a grave man in his sixties, of some humour and sophistication*	Judge at the witch trials in Salem and other parts of Massachusetts; signs the death sentences

21

2 The Crucible

Character	Quotation	Description
4.	in his sixties, a bitter, remorseless Salem judge	Judge in the Salem court
5.	a strikingly beautiful girl, an orphan, with an endless capacity for dissembling	A vengeful, manipulative liar; she starts the proceedings in Salem by lying about what has happened
6.	aged ten	Reverend Parris' daughter; one of the "hysterical" girls
7.	a nervous, hurried girl	Works for Dr Griggs; one of the "hysterical" girls
8.	a fat, sly, merciless girl of eighteen	The Putnams' servant; one of the "hysterical" girls; runs away with Abigail when things go wrong
9.	seventeen, a subservient, naïve, lonely girl.	The Proctors' servant; one of the "hysterical" girls; admits she was lying but is then scared into joining the hysterical girls again
10.	a negro slave, in her forties	Reverend Parris' black slave; said to be able to talk to the dead
11.		John Proctor's wife; victim; tries to forgive her husband
12.	a twisted soul of forty-five, a death-ridden woman, haunted by dreams	Believes a witch killed her seven babies; accuses Rebecca Nurse of witchcraft
13.	a farmer in his middle thirties; powerful of body, even-tempered and not easily led	Farmer in Salem; had an affair with Abigail; feels guilty; in the end rediscovers his lost goodness and saves his name
14.	eighty-three; He is knotted with muscle, canny, inquisitive, and still powerful	Mistakenly makes people think his wife is a witch; tries to defend her in court; killed by having weights put on his chest
15.	seventy-two; She is white-haired, leaning upon her walking-stick	Highly respected villager in Salem; very kind and charitable; argues against the witch trial proceedings; accused of witchcraft
16.	he was called upon to arbitrate disputes as though he were an unofficial judge	Farmer and landowner; respected and often asked to help sort out disputes
17.	a well-to-do, hard-handed landowner, near fifty; vindictive nature, man with many grievances	Greedy landowner; accuses his neighbours of witchcraft so he can buy their land after their execution
18.		Clerk of the court; brings the warrant for Elizabeth's arrest
19.	a man in his early thirties	Appointed by the court to arrest those accused of witchcraft

The Crucible | 2

c) *As you read through the play, choose one of these characters – John Proctor, Abigail Williams, Elizabeth Proctor or Reverend Parris – and make notes on them.*
You will need this information a little later, so make sure you take notes carefully. →S11

TIP

Bookmark. Fold a piece of paper in half and on one half note down important quotations (made by them or another character about them) and on the other, your thoughts on what they do and say. Use this piece of paper as a bookmark so that you can jot things down easily as you read the play.

Act One, Part One

3 *Read the opening of Act One, up to the point where John Proctor enters. Then read the statements below and put the letter of the correct answer into the box below.*

1. Abigail Williams is Parris'
    a) niece.
    b) step-daughter.
    c) servant.

2. The person who believes that there might be an "unnatural cause" to Betty's illness is
    a) Reverend Parris.
    b) Abigail.
    c) Doctor Griggs.

3. Susanna is sent home and told not to
    a) tell anyone that Betty is ill.
    b) spread any rumours of witchcraft.
    c) tell anyone that Doctor Griggs cannot help Betty.

4. Reverend Parris had caught the girls
    a) conjuring spirits in the forest.
    b) killing animals in the forest.
    c) dancing in the forest.

5. Abigail says she no longer works for Goody Proctor because
    a) she did not want to be a servant.
    b) Goody Proctor dislikes her and wanted her to work too hard.
    c) she was asked to work for another family.

6. Reverend Parris has sent for Reverend Hale because
    a) Hale has a lot of experience with witches and evil.
    b) he is convinced there are witches in Salem.
    c) Ruth Putnam is also sick.

7. Thomas Putnam is described by the narrator as being
    a) full of resentment, bitter and wanting revenge.
    b) bitter, poor and intellectually superior to most of the people around him.
    c) not very interested in what goes on in the parish and full of his own importance.

8. Ann Putnam sent her daughter Ruth to see Tituba
    a) to find out who killed Ruth's babies as Tituba can conjure up the dead.
    b) to bring back Ann's dead babies as Tituba can do magic.
    c) to find out who killed Ann's babies as Tituba can speak to the dead.

9. Mary Warren says they have to tell the truth because
    a) people are saying the girls are witches, and the punishment for this is being whipped.
    b) farmers are saying the girls are witches, and the punishment for this is hanging.
    c) Tituba is saying the girls are witches, and the punishment for this is being whipped.

10. Abigail forbids the other girls from saying that
    a) she drank a charm to kill Elizabeth Proctor.
    b) Tituba conjured up Ruth's dead sisters.
    c) she saw Indians smash her parents' heads on the pillow.

2 | The Crucible

TIP

The opening scene of a film is particularly important because it sets the tone and has to hook the audience. It might also introduce important themes and have dramatic foreshadowing of the events to come.
For this task refer to the special skill on the visual aspects of film that your teacher will give you.

4 a) [👥] **Viewing:** Now watch the opening of the film on DVD. In groups of four, each of you should answer **one** of the questions in the space provided below. →S29

1. On whom is our attention focused in the opening scene? How is this done?
2. Why do we see the dancing scene? How does this affect how we view the rest of the scene?
3. What important themes does it introduce and does it contain any dramatic foreshadowing?
4. How do the setting, lighting, colours and soundtrack help to set the tone?

_____
_____
_____
_____
_____
_____
_____
_____
_____
_____

TIP

In the author's note to the screenplay, Miller wrote "plays worked away at revealing an *idea*. Movies did not have an idea they had action."

b) **Presentation:** Present your ideas to the rest of the group and answer any questions they might have. →S22

c) [👥] **Discussion:** In your groups discuss why you think Miller chose to change the opening scene for the film – his explanation on the left might give you a hint. Think about which version you prefer – the play or film – and why. Be prepared to justify your ideas! →S26

Act One, Part Two

5 Now continue reading Act One until Reverend Hale enters. Then read through the statements below. Decide whether each one is true or false. Find a quotation in the text to support your decision and note it down in the right-hand column. →S11

	True	False	Quotation
Proctor warns Abigail that she's going to get into trouble.			
Abigail tells Proctor that his wife is saying bad things about her in the village.			
Proctor wants to continue his affair with Abigail.			
When Betty hears people singing a hymn downstairs she wakes up and starts laughing.			
Giles Corey has heard that Betty is singing psalms.			
Rebecca Nurse thinks that Ruth and Betty are up to childish pranks and that Ruth will soon wake up.			

	True	False	Quotation
John Proctor has asked Reverend Hale to come to Salem.			
Reverend Parris says that Hale is coming to look for devils in the village.			
Rebecca says that Reverend Parris should send Hale away as his presence will only cause arguments.			
People in the village are staying away from church because Reverend Parris only talks about hell.			
Reverend Parris does not think he is paid enough money and believes that he is treated badly.			
John Proctor does not speak freely in front of Reverend Parris.			
Mr Putnam accuses John Proctor of taking wood from his land.			

6 [👥] **Discussion:** *Think about why this part is crucial for the development of the plot. Briefly discuss your ideas in class.* →S26

Act One, Part Three

7 *Finish reading Act One. Read through the statements below and find the corresponding quotation in the text that shows the truth of each statement.* →S11

1. Reverend Hale has recently discovered a witch.
   _____

2. Reverend Hale has heard good things about Rebecca Nurse.
   _____

3. Proctor tells Hale that he has never said whether he believes in witches or not before.
   _____

4. Mrs Putnam tells Reverend Hale that Tituba has been known to talk with spirits.
   _____

5. Without meaning to, Giles Corey suggests to Hale that his wife might be involved with witchcraft.
   _____

6. People often say it is Giles Corey's fault if bad things happen in the village.
   _____

7. After Reverend Hale asks Abigail what she is hiding from him, she denies that she has any connection with the Devil.
   _____

2 | The Crucible

8. Abigail accuses Tituba of bewitching her in church and making her do inappropriate things there.
   _____

9. Tituba says she cannot wake Betty.
   _____

10. Tituba claims that there are other witches working for the Devil.
    _____

11. Reverend Hale tells Tituba not to be afraid to confess who else is involved because the Devil cannot harm him as he is a minister.
    _____

12. Tituba says that the Devil told her to kill Reverend Parris because he is not a good man.
    _____

8 [👥] **Discussion:** *Think about why Abigail and the other girls start joining in and "confessing" at the end of Act One. Discuss your ideas with a partner.* →S26

Act Two

9 *Once you have read Act Two, summarise the action by numbering the statements in the order that these events occur. The first one has been given to get you started, but be careful, there is one statement that you do not need.*

_1_	It is now eight days later and the setting is the Proctors' farmhouse.
__	Reverend Hale comes to tell them that Elizabeth has been accused in court.
__	Mary Warren says that she saved Elizabeth's life after she was accused in court.
__	John tells Reverend Hale that Abigail has told him that the children's sickness had nothing to do with witchcraft.
__	Elizabeth says there is now a "proper" court in Salem with judges from Boston.
__	Cheever discovers a needle in the stomach of Elizabeth's poppet.
__	Giles Corey and Francis Nurse arrive to say that their wives have been taken.
__	John says that vengeance is is behind all of the events in Salem.
__	Mary gives Elizabeth a poppet she made for her during the day's proceedings.
__	John recites the Ten Commandments, forgetting the one about adultery.
__	Cheever arrives to arrest Elizabeth.
__	Elizabeth asks John to talk to Abigail. She believes that Abigail wants her dead so she can marry John.
__	Elizabeth leaves with Herrick and Cheever.
__	Elizabeth tells her husband that Mary Warren has gone to Salem.
__	Abigail was found stabbed that night with a needle in her stomach.
__	John says he's taking Mary to the court to explain how the poppet came to their house.
__	Mary says her work at the court is important because the Devil is loose in Salem.
__	Elizabeth tells John he should go and warn the court that Abigail is telling lies.
__	John rips up the arrest warrant for his wife despite protests.
__	Cheevers asks whether Elizabeth has any poppets in the house.
__	Elizabeth tells John that she believes she will never see him again.
__	Elizabeth is afraid that Abigail wants her dead and that Abigail will continue to accuse her until she is arrested.

The Crucible | 2

10 *What would we call a "poppet" in modern-day English? Why is Cheever looking for one in Elizabeth's house? What is its significance? Note down your ideas in the space provided below.*

_____

_____

_____

_____

Act Three

11 *Put a cross next to the right word, depending on whether the characters are telling lies or the truth. There are two statement containing things that are not said at all.* →S11

1. Giles Corey tells the court that the girls are lying. Lie____ Truth____
2. Reverend Hale says that Rebecca Nurse has been condemned to death that morning. Lie____ Truth____
3. When first questioned by Danforth, Mary claims that she never saw any spirits and that the girls are lying. Lie____ Truth____
4. Cheever tells Danforth that Proctor damned the court when his wife was arrested. Lie____ Truth____
5. Reverend Parris says that Proctor has come because his wife is pregnant. Lie____ Truth____
6. John Proctor tells Danforth that his wife never lies. Lie____ Truth____
7. Mary admits to Danforth that she sat in his court lying, even though she knew that her evidence would cause people to be hanged. Lie____ Truth____
8. When Abigail is told of Mary's confession, she says that Mary is lying. Lie____ Truth____
9. Abigail says that Goody Proctor always kept poppets at her house. Lie____ Truth____
10. Mary says she does not want to faint in court again. Lie____ Truth____
11. John Proctor tells the court that he has slept with Abigail. Lie____ Truth____
12. Elizabeth Proctor tells the court that her husband John has never committed adultery. Lie____ Truth____
13. Reverend Hale tells Danforth that he has always distrusted Abigail. Lie____ Truth____
14. At the end Mary takes back what she previously said, claiming that John Proctor is the Devil's man and made her sign the Devil's Book. Lie____ Truth____

12 [👥] **Discussion:** *Elizabeth is called in to the court to find out whether her husband is lying or not. How are her words used against him? Is this fair? Why, why not? Discuss your ideas with a partner.* →S26

Act Four

13 *Read Act Four and choose the correct answer(s) to the question below. There might be more than one correct answer – so tick all the ones that apply.* →S11

1. What does Mr. Parris say has happened to his niece?
   - ☐ a) Abigail has vanished with Mercy Lewis.
   - ☐ b) Abigail has stolen all of his money.
   - ☐ c) Abigail has gone to Andover.

2. Why does Mr Parris suggest delaying the hangings?
   - ☐ a) The villagers might riot if good people are hanged.
   - ☐ b) He has been threatened and is worried that he might be murdered.
   - ☐ c) Mr Hale has just got some of the prisoners to confess to witchcraft.

27

The Crucible

3. Deputy Governor Danforth says he cannot pardon the prisoners or postpone the hangings. Why?
   - [ ] a) It would not be fair as others have already been executed for the same crime.
   - [ ] b) He is afraid to pardon them.
   - [ ] c) Their names have been publicly announced and the villagers expect them to die.

4. What do we learn about the situation in Salem?
   - [ ] a) Orphans are being forced to live in the next village.
   - [ ] b) Cows are wandering around without any owners.
   - [ ] c) People live in fear wondering when the girls will accuse them of witchcraft.

5. What does Reverend Hale tell Elizabeth Proctor?
   - [ ] a) He is going to murder her husband.
   - [ ] b) He tells her not to make her husband lie as he is a good man.
   - [ ] c) He asks her to persuade her husband to confess, even though this is a lie.

6. What has happened to Giles Corey?
   - [ ] a) He was hanged.
   - [ ] b) He confessed to ensure his sons were given his farm.
   - [ ] c) He refused to confess and refused to deny the charges against him.

7. What does John say to Elizabeth?
   - [ ] a) He is thinking of confessing.
   - [ ] b) He has not confessed because he does not respect the authorities.
   - [ ] c) He is never going to confess because the others have not confessed.

8. Why does John say "I speak my own sins; I cannot judge another" (**139**/1)?
   - [ ] a) He is not a judge so is not allowed to pass judgement on anyone else.
   - [ ] b) He does not want to condemn anyone else.
   - [ ] c) He has been forbidden from condemning anyone else.

9. Why does John change his mind and take back his confession?
   - [ ] a) His confession will make his children suffer.
   - [ ] b) He does not want to blacken his name as this is all he has left.
   - [ ] c) He will not sign a lie when the others refuse to lie and are going to be hanged.

10. Elizabeth says at the end "He have his goodness now. God forbid I take it from him" (**142**/15-16) What does she mean?
    - [ ] a) He has confessed to God and is now good again. She will not take it away from him by making a fuss.
    - [ ] b) He is going to his death peacefully and she will not go and upset him by crying.
    - [ ] c) He has made the right and moral decision (not to lie) and she will not stop him by trying to make him confess.

14 *Discussion:* When Deputy Governor Danforth hears that Proctor is going to confess, he says:

[with great relief and gratitude] Praise to God, man, praise to God; you shall be blessed in Heaven for this. (**136**/22-23)

In small groups answer the following questions, making notes in the space provided, and discuss Danforth's reaction. → S26

1. Why does he react like this?
   _____

2. What does this show us about the purpose of the trials?
   _____

3. Why does Danforth have to hang Proctor in the end?
   _____

The Crucible | 2

15 a) *Writing:* Imagine you are a journalist who has been attending the Salem witch trials. It is the day after Proctor's death and you are going to write a short article summarising what has happened. You may either choose one of the following headlines or invent one of your own. →S17

Dark deeds in Massachusetts

Leave me my name!

Salem's shame

Exclusive: Proctor confesses!

b) *Writing:* Once you have chosen your headline, start by making notes on the five Ws below and thinking about what information you need to include and what you can leave out. →S17

Who?
_____
_____
_____
_____
_____

What?
_____
_____
_____
_____
_____

Where?
_____
_____
_____
_____
_____

When?
_____
_____
_____
_____
_____

Why?
_____
_____
_____
_____
_____

TIP

Which type of newspaper do you write for?
tabloid: focuses on the human interest angle; presents facts more subjectively and emotionally
quality: presents facts more neutrally

TIP

Remember the **ABC** of news writing: **A**ccuracy (the facts have to be correct), **B**revity (keep to the point) and **C**larity (keep it simple so that everyone can understand what you are saying). In addition you will need to answer the five Ws: **W**ho? **W**hat? **W**here? **W**hen? **W**hy?

2 | The Crucible

Additional Information
_____
_____
_____
_____
_____
_____
_____

> **TIP**
>
> Remember to follow the pyramid structure: start with the most important information and, then add more facts and additional details, ending with the least important information at the end.

c) **Writing:** *Write your report on a separate piece of paper.* →S17
d) [👥] *Now check your work! Once you have read it through, exchange your article with that of your neighbour and peer edit each other's work (using a pencil).* →S19, →S20

16 [👥] **Discussion:** *In pairs speculate as to whether the witch-hunt in Salem was caused by Abigail. If she and the other girls had not been caught dancing, do you think the witch-hunt would still have taken place?*
[👥👥] *Collect ideas for both sides of the argument below and then have a mobile debate in class.*
→S26

> **TIP**
>
> **Mobile debate**
> In this kind of debate, you physically move from one side of the classroom to the other to show which side you support. The motion (topic) is written on the board and underneath this on one side the word "for" and on the other the word "against". Before the debate begins, the pupils decide whether they agree with (so are "for") or disagree with ("against") the motion and move to that side of the room. After this, each pupil gives an argument to support their side of the case. If an argument is particularly persuasive, the pupils are allowed to change sides once that speaker has finished presenting their argument.

For
_____
_____
_____
_____
_____
_____
_____
_____
_____
_____
_____

Against
_____
_____
_____
_____
_____
_____
_____
_____
_____
_____

The Crucible | 2

C Analysis

1 [👥] *"The Crucible" follows the traditional* **five stages of a tragedy:** *exposition – rising action – climax – falling action – dénouement. In pairs discuss which part of the play falls into which stage and label the diagram below. Once you have finished, compare your diagram with that of the pair sitting next to you.* →S5

```
                    climax

    rising action                  falling action


  exposition                         dénouement
```

2 a) *Where do we usually find the word "overture"? Why do you think Miller gives this subtitle to Act One.*

b) [👥👥] **Discussion:** *Divide into small groups and think about what subtitles could be given to Acts II, III and IV. Decide on the best one in each case and write them on the board. Discuss.* →S26

Act II: _____
_____
_____
_____

Act III: _____
_____
_____
_____

Act IV: _____
_____
_____
_____

USEFUL PHRASES

From the end of Act XX when … says/-confesses/…

From the opening of Act XX when we

… through to/up to/ to the beginning of Act XX when …

… to …'s decision/ lie/-confession/ admission

In Act XX when …

3 a) [👥] *Miller added Act Two Scene 2 in 1972 but removed it again a little later. Some critics have said that it is neither necessary dramatically nor thematically. Once you have read Act Two Scene II, note down your thoughts below. Then compare them with those of your neighbour.*

Good / helpful	Not necessary
_____	_____
_____	_____
_____	_____

31

2 | The Crucible

b) [👥] **Discussion:** *The actor Laurence Olivier once told Miller that Act Two Scene Two destroys the play's underlying "drumbeat" and "marching tempo". What do you think? Does this change any of the ideas you had above? Discuss your ideas in class.* →S26

4 a) **Vocabulary:** *Focus on the play's title and look up the definition of the word "crucible" in your dictionary. What is the literal meaning? How is a crucible used? What other meaning can it have? Note down your findings in the space below.* →S3

Literal meaning: _____
_____
_____
_____

How is it used: _____
_____
_____
_____

Other meaning: _____
_____
_____
_____

> **TIP**
> When you have formed your groups, decide which group(s) is/are going to deal with which character. All four should be dealt with by at least one group.

b) [👥] *In small groups, choose one of the following characters and think about how the term "crucible" relates to their particular situation:*

| John Proctor | Elizabeth Proctor | Giles Cory | Reverend Hale |

First of all brainstorm your ideas in the space below.

c) [👥] *Share your ideas with the others in your group. Decide how you are going to display them on a poster. You should include quotations to support your ideas. If you wish, use visual information (e.g stills from the film, photographs from a production etc.)* →S31

The Crucible | 2

d) [👥] **Vocabulary:** Then choose one of the adjectives from the list below that you think best sums up their actions in their "crucible" situation as a heading for your poster. If you prefer, you may also choose a different adjective but be prepared to justify your choice!

upright	sad	moving	passive	courageous
heroic	hypocritical	virtuous	blameless	cold
disillusioned	tortured	strong	defiant	honorable
broken	sincere			

e) **Presentation:** Once you have finished, put your results up on the classroom wall. One person from each group should stay with your poster to answer any questions while the others walk around and look at the other results. Make sure that everyone has a chance to look around!
→ S22

5 a) [👥] *As in real life, some of the characters are closer to each other than others. Look at the characters in the box and think about their relationships according to what we learn in Act One.*

> Abigail – Tituba – Susanna – Betty – Mercy – Reverend Parris – Thomas Putnam – Ann Putnam – Rebecca Nurse – Giles Corey – Reverend Hale

As the protagonist, John Proctor is in the centre.
If a character is close to John Proctor, write his/her name close to John's. Group together the ones who are actually close or get on well with each other and put a circle around the characters that form a group.
Compare your diagram with that of your neighbour, justifying your decisions if necessary.
→ S7

John Proctor

2 | The Crucible

b) [👥] Now do the same for the characters in Act Three. What has changed? You will need to add the characters from the box here.

> Elizabeth Proctor – Francis Nurse – Ezekiel Cheever – Judge Hathorne – Deputy Governor Danforth

Proceed as above.

6 a) *Vocabulary:* Look at this list of words that can be used to characterise people. Look up any words you are not sure about in your dictionary. →S3

a_ ambitious	e_ easy-going	l_ loyal	sensitive
ashamed	envious	m_ manipulative	steadfast
c_ caring	f_ faithful	moral	strong-willed
charming	foolish	n_ naïve	t_ tense
cheerful	forgiving	o_ outspoken	triumphant
cold	h_ honest	p_ passionate	troubled
confident	honorable	passive	trusting
courageous	hurtful	proud	u_ unbalanced
cruel	hypocritical	r_ rational	v_ vindictive
d_ desperate	hysterical	remorseless	virtuous
destructive	i_ impulsive	ruthless	vulnerable
devout	intelligent	s_ self-confident	w_ weak
dominating	j_ jealous	selfish	wild

b) [👥] You have been gathering information on one of the following characters – John Proctor, Abigail Williams, Elizabeth Proctor, Reverend Parris – and putting it on your bookmark. Decide which adjectives apply to him or her during the play. Find a quotation to support your answer – the information that you have been gathering will be of help. Note down your findings below.

The Crucible | 2

Character:

Adjective	Quotation
_____	_____
_____	_____
_____	_____
_____	_____
_____	_____
_____	_____
_____	_____
_____	_____
_____	_____
_____	_____
_____	_____

c) *Then explain your choices to a partner.* →S7

d) **Writing:** *Characterise the person you have chosen. Remember to support your points with suitable quotations from the play. Write about 200 words on a separate piece of paper.* →S7

7 a) *Several of the characters undergo a change in the play, but Reverend Hale undergoes the greatest transition: from accusing, to sympathising with and finally defending the innocent. Read the changes Reverend Hale goes through below (a – l). Put them in the correct order (left box).*

order		Act
☐	a) Starts arguing in favour of the accused.	☐
☐	b) Begs Elizabeth to change John's mind as he sees the trials are senseless.	☐
☐	c) Pleads on behalf of the accused.	☐
☐	d) Denounces the proceedings of the court.	☐
☐	e) Wants to find out what the Proctors are really like.	☐
☐	f) Confident he will be able to fight the devil.	☐
☐	g) Is exhausted and drained by the proceedings.	☐
☐	h) Starts questioning the court's judgement.	☐
☐	i) Arrives in Salem with good intentions.	☐
☐	j) First hears of the suspicions that Abigail is a liar.	☐
☐	k) Initiates the proceedings by getting Tituba to confess.	☐
☐	l) Goes to the Proctors' house of his own accord.	☐

b) *Now assign them to the correct Act (right box).*

2 | The Crucible

c) *Now decide which of the adjectives below best describe him in each Act (some of them might be appropriate for more than one Act) and put them in the table.*

broken	curious	disillusioned	naive	frantic
(over)confident	self-important	sincere	tortured	angry
troubled	uncertain	exhausted		

Act I	Act II	Act III	Act IV

d) **Writing:** *Using the information above, outline the transformation that Reverend Hale undergoes in a short text of about 200 words. Write it on a separate piece of paper.* →S7

The Witch House in Salem, Massachusetts

8 [👥👥👥] **Online presentation:** *In groups, choose either Abigail or Elizabeth and think about how they might present themselves on a social networking site today. Think about what interests they might have, contacts etc. Note down your ideas below and put together their profile, either on the computer or as a poster. Show your results to the rest of the class and contrast the two different profiles.* →S23

_____
_____
_____
_____
_____
_____
_____
_____

9 a) *Abigail, Elizabeth and Mr Parris have been invited to talk about what happened after the event. Imagine they are taking part in a chat show. What questions would the chat show host ask? What questions might the audience want to ask? Make notes below.*

Interviewer: _____
_____
_____
_____
_____
_____
_____

Audience: _____
_____

The Crucible | 2

_____
_____
_____
_____
_____
_____
_____
_____

b) [👥] **Role play:** *In groups of four, each of you should take on one of the roles (Abigail, Elizabeth, Mr Parris, chat show host) and decide which questions you want to ask and how each character is going to react. Then act out the role play in front of the class. The rest of the class is the audience and should be allowed to ask questions at the end that the characters should also answer.* → S24

10 a) [👥] *Divide into small groups. Each group should choose one of the following language features:*

- Unusual syntax and constructions
- Old-fashioned language
- Biblical language
- Black and white images

b) *Find at least two examples of your language feature in the play. Translate each into modern English, then look at how it is used, what effect it creates on a modern-day audience and think about why Miller might have used it.* → S33

Example 1

Quote: _____
_____
_____

Translation: _____
_____
_____
_____

How used: _____
_____
_____
_____

Effect: _____
_____
_____
_____

Why used: _____
_____
_____
_____

37

2 | The Crucible

Example 2

Quote: _____

Translation: _____

How used: _____

Effect: _____

Why used: _____

c) **Discussion:** *Once you have done the tasks above, form new groups of four with one representative for each of the language features. Then share and discuss your findings with the rest of the group.* →S26

11 a) Presentation: *Miller uses different imagery in the play. Read through the following quotations and, in pairs, choose one of them and make notes on its meaning in the space below. Remember to put the quote into context by outlining which character says it, and why.*

1. "There are wheels within wheels in this village and fires within fires" (Act I) (**38**/25-26)

2. "Why, Rebecca, we may open up the boil of all our troubles today!" (Act I) (**50**/18-19)

3. "Now the little crazy children are jangling the keys of the kingdom, and common vengeance writes the law!" (Act II) (**84**/12-13)

4. "Oh Elizabeth your justice would freeze beer!" (Act II) (**64**/17-18)

5. "This is a sharp time, now, a precise time – we live no longer in the dusky afternoon when evil mixed itself with good and befuddled the world." (Act III) (**98**/11-13)

6. "We burn a hot fire here; it melts down all concealment." (Act III) (**93**/23)

7. "I came into this village like a bridegroom to his beloved, bearing gifts of high religion; the very crowns of holy law I brought, and what I touched with my bright confidence, it died; and where I turned the eye of my great faith, blood flowed up." (Act IV) (**130**/28-29)

8. "For now I do think I see some shred of goodness in John Proctor. Not enough to weave a banner with, but white enough to keep it from such dogs." (Act IV) (**141**/18-20)

The Witch Museum in Salem, Massachusetts

b) **Presentation:** *Now explain its meaning to the rest of the class.*

12 a) *One of the central themes in "The Crucible" is "conflict".*
Choose one of the aspects in the tipbox, writing which one it is in the circle below and note down your ideas and examples. Add additional arrows if necessary. Remember to find examples in the text to justify your choices!
[👥] *Once you have finished compare your findings with someone else who chose the same example as you did.*

TIP

Miller presents different aspects of the theme "conflict" in his play:
- some characters have to deal with **internal conflicts,**
- there are **external conflicts** within the community
- and, of course, **conflicts between** different **characters** and **within relationships.**

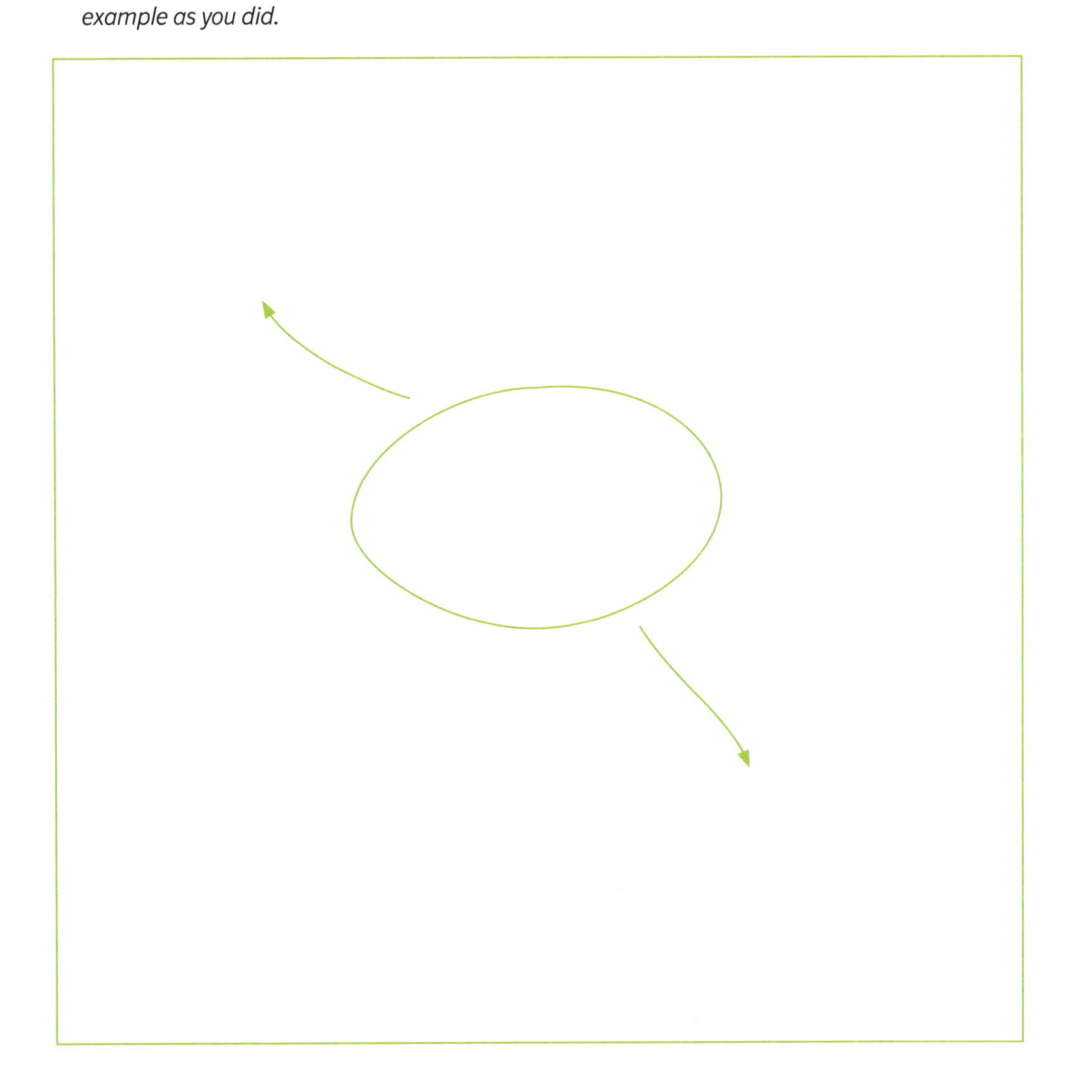

b) **Presentation/Discussion:** *Form groups with at least one example of each type of conflict and present your findings to the others. Discuss what Miller is trying to say about what conflict can do to a community and an individual.* →S22

2 | The Crucible

13 a) [👥] *Discussion:* Which of the following universal literary themes are central to "The Crucible"? Discuss in pairs, note the themes down and find quotations to support your ideas.

revenge	true love	ambition	madness
prejudice	pride	intolerance	man against nature
good and evil	family	greed	power
coming of age	betrayal	death	loss
friendship	faith	hate	loyalty
search for knowledge			

Themes	Quotations

b) [👥] *Discussion:* If you had to choose one theme to sum up the events in the play, which one would it be, and why?
Note down your thoughts in the space provided below and discuss your choice with your neighbour.

c) *Writing:* Write a theme paragraph (about 150 words) on your chosen theme on a separate piece of paper. Remember to check your work once you have finished! →S14

14 a) [👥] *Brainstorm / Discussion:* What motif would you use to advertise a production of "The Crucible"? In groups, brainstorm your ideas, thinking which one best sums up what the play is about. →S31

b) *Presentation:* Search for different playbills for "The Crucible" online and make a note of the motifs used to advertise the play. Present the one that you find most appealing to the class, giving reasons for your answer. If you prefer, you could design your own playbill instead, but be prepared to justified your choice of motif. →S26

The Crucible | 2

D Further activities

1 [👥] ***Internet research:*** *Research the relationship between Miller and McCarthyism in small groups.*
Choose one of the following topics and find out more about it on the Internet. Then prepare a short presentation (5 minutes) on your chosen topic for the rest of the class. →S22, →S32

- The Cold War
- Senator Joseph McCarthy – biography
- Miller and the HUAC
- McCarthyism in America
- The House Un-American Activities Committee (HUAC)

> **TIP**
> Make sure that everyone in the group presents a small part of the information.

2 ***Listening:*** *The following interview is about the McCarthy witch-hunts in Hollywood in the 1950s.*
You will hear the interview twice.
Listen to the interview and answer the questions, in 1 to 6 words.
You will then hear the interview again.
After the second listening you will have another 60 seconds to complete your answers. →S21

1. How does the interviewer describe the McCarthy witch-hunts at the beginning?

2. How does she describe the search that took place?

3. What reasons does Amanda Foreman say were the basis for people being accused of being a "card-carrying communist"?

4. What destroyed the movie stars' careers?

5. In Michael Friedland's story about the accused movie star, what does he say she was supposed to do to save her career?

6. Why does Amanda Foreman say it was a good decision for her father not to give up names? It was good for him as …

7. What two qualities does Amanda say are necessary to do what her father did?
    1.
    2.

8. What did the events turn Amanda's father into?

9. How long were many people members of the Communist Party?

10. What two reasons does Michael Friedland give as to why people joined the Communist Party?

2 | The Crucible

FACT FILE

Arthur Miller wrote *The Crucible* at the height of Senator McCarthy's hearings in the 1950s. It was intended as a metaphor for what was going on in the US at the time, and more broadly to show how intolerance and hysteria can tear apart a community.

3 [👥] *Discussion:* What parallels can you find between McCarthyism in the US and the events in Miller's play? Make notes in the table below and discuss your findings with a partner.

McCarthyism in the US	The Crucible

4 *Writing:* "A witch-hunt like the one described in Arthur Miller's play could not happen in modern-day society." Comment on this statement (on a separate piece of paper). →S14

5 *Mediation:* You have been doing a project with your partner school in Britain on dangers posed by the Internet. You decide to give the main points/arguments of this article from the *Süddeutsche Zeitung* to your partner school. Write in the space below the article. →S33

TIP

Read the article and highlight key words and phrases. Then think of how you can sum up these points in English. When you are doing so, remember to be careful to avoid interference with the German, both as far as grammatical constructions are concerned as well as vocabulary items.

Hexenjagd im Internet

Der Albtraum des Internetzeitalters: Chinas neuester Volkssport heißt „Cyber-Stalking" – Menschen werden online denunziert und fertiggemacht.

Die Hexenjagd gegen Yin Qi ist in vollem Gange. Der 31-jährige Pekinger erlebt gerade den Albtraum des Internetzeitalters: Irgendjemandem gefiel
5 sein Privatleben nicht. Yin wurde im Internet öffentlich an den Pranger gestellt.
Und schon rufen Tausende wütende Chinesen bei seinem Chef an und ver-
10 langen, dass er gefeuert wird.
Der Abteilungsleiter in der Pekinger Niederlassung der britischen Firma Quantel, einem Hersteller von digitaler TV-Ausrüstung, ist das jüngste Opfer
15 eines neuen chinesischen Volkssportes: Cyber-Stalking. Selbsternannte Moralapostel oder Patrioten suchen sich einen unglücklichen Zeitgenossen aus, fällen öffentlich ihr Urteil über ihn und
20 fallen dann gemeinsam über ihn her.
Yins Probleme begannen, als seine Ehefrau Zhang Meiran im Internet über seine Exfrau herzog. Unter dem Tarnnamen „Candy" machte sich die neue
25 Ehefrau in recht gehässiger Weise über die geschiedene Ehefrau lustig. Die Ex hatte bei ihrer Scheidung von Yin die gemeinsame Wohnung erhalten, was der neuen Ehefrau offenbar nicht passte. „Sie ist nur eine billige Henne, 30 die beim Sex nur eine einzige Position kennt", schrieb Zhang Meiran alias „Candy" in ihrem Blog.
Das war nicht nett, zugegeben. Doch was darauf folgte, war schlimmer und 35 gehässiger. Erst Hunderte, dann Tausende und Zehntausende begannen, sich im Internet über das Ehepaar Yin und Zhang aufzuregen. „Und du glaubst, du bist hübsch? Schau dir dein 40 Gesicht an, flach wie ein indischer Pfannkuchen", schrieb einer an Candys Adresse.
Yin Qi sei unmoralisch, weil er schon während seiner ersten Ehe ein Verhält- 45 nis mit Zhang Meiran hatte, befanden die selbsternannten Moralwächter im Internet. Irgendjemand wühlte so lange, bis die Namen des Ehepaars, ihre Personalausweisnummern, Adressen 50 und Telefonnummern bekannt waren. All dies - gemeinsam mit Fotos des Paares - wurde ins Internet gestellt. Seither laufen im Büro von Yins Firma in

Peking alle Telefone heiß. Die Anrufer verlangen, dass die Firma den Chinesen entlässt. „Wie können Sie solch einen Menschen beschäftigen", brüllen sie durch den Hörer. „Wir bekommen jede Menge ärgerliche Anrufe wegen Yin Qi", bestätigte eine Mitarbeiterin von Quantel am Montag auf Nachfrage. Der zur Zielscheibe gewordene Yin Qi muss sich verleugnen lassen.

Solche an die Kulturrevolution erinnernden Hexenjagden, die aus dem Internet ins reale Leben übergreifen, sind in China häufig geworden. Vergangenes Jahr verlangten Tausende Surfer, dem Liebhaber einer verheirateten Frau „den Kopf abzuschlagen". Der junge Mann mit dem Internet-Namen „bronzefarbener Schnurrbart" musste sich verstecken. Auch telefonische Morddrohungen gegen Ausländer sind vorgekommen, denen „Beleidigung der chinesischen Nation" vorgeworfen wurde.

Henrik Bork in der *Süddeutschen Zeitung*, 22.05.2010

Chapter 3 *My Son the Fanatic*

A Introduction

1 a) **Viewing:** Watch the opening sequence of "East is East". The sequence runs for about 10 minutes. Then read the statements and put the letter of the correct answer into the box below.

1. Ella Khan tells her friend Annie that
   a) her husband has come back from the Mosque early.
   b) her children must leave the procession immediately.
   c) her children must put on masks.
   d) there will be a party at their house after the procession.

2. Ella's daughter Meenah complains to her mother that
   a) she is doing her hair in the wrong way.
   b) her little brother Sajid is calling her names.
   c) they don't have a proper bathroom in the house.
   d) they will be late for the wedding.

3. When George Khan gives his son Nazir a watch, he tells him that
   a) it is a wedding present.
   b) it is a family watch that is given to the eldest son at his wedding.
   c) it is a present from his grandmother.
   d) his name is engraved on the watch in Arabic.

4. When the Khans' British neighbour watches the Khans getting into the minibus, he speaks of
   a) a circus in the area.
   b) a "piccaninnies' picnic".
   c) a great and colourful ceremony.
   d) a stupid show of costumes.

5. When Nazir abruptly leaves the wedding ceremony he tells his father that
   a) he picked the wrong woman for him.
   b) he doesn't like the bride.
   c) he can't go ahead with the ceremony.
   d) he is ill and must go outside.

44

6. Asking the local Mullah why his son has brought shame to the family, George Khan is told that
   a) the children of mixed marriages are different.
   b) they are more British than Pakistani.
   c) it was wrong to have married a white English woman.
   d) it was wrong to have arranged his son's marriage.

1. ☐ 2. ☐ 3. ☐ 4. ☐ 5. ☐ 6. ☐ 7. ☐ 8. ☐

b) **Viewing:** *After the second viewing note down to what extent George Khan, the first generation immigrant, has adapted to British culture? Consider, for example, his marriage to Ella or his seeking advice from the local Mullah.*

_____
_____
_____
_____
_____
_____
_____
_____

c) **Writing:** *Describe the relationship between father and children.*

_____
_____
_____
_____
_____
_____
_____
_____

2 Reading: *Read the text "It's no use pointing the finger at ethnic minorities". on pages 100/101 in* **Green Line Oberstufe Niedersachsen.** *The text is about the concepts of integration vs. multiculturalism/segregation and the respective attitudes that go with each concept. Then do the following tasks.*

a) *Collect words and phrases from the text that refer to either concept.* →S11

Integration	multiculturalism
_____	_____
_____	_____
_____	_____
_____	_____

b) *Explain the underlying assumption of each concept. What does each presuppose?*

Integration	multiculturalism
_____	_____
_____	_____
_____	_____
_____	_____

3 | My Son the Fanatic

c) *Analyse the writer's use of the patchwork metaphor.*

d) *Summarise in your own words the writer's view of multiculturalism.* → S13

e) *Speculate on the problems that may arise in a family of first and second generation ethnic minorities with regard to adopting the values of British mainstream society.*

3 **Reading** Read the text on pages 102/103 in **Green Line Oberstufe Niedersachsen** "Britain should integrate into Muslim values". The text is about three generations of Muslim families in Britain, the changes in the relationship between parents and children and the role of the Muslim community. Then do the following tasks.

a) *Collect words and phrases that refer to the three different generations of Muslim families.*

First generation:

Second generation:

Third generation:

My Son the Fanatic | 3

b) *Point out the major differences between the second and third generation.*

c) *Discuss the terms "integration" and "multiculturalism" with regard to the second and third generation.*

d) *Comment on the writer's criticism of the third generation.* → S14

TIP

You are expected to deal with tasks 3b – d in the following way:
Think: jot down your individual thoughts
Pair: Exchange your ideas with your partner
Share: get together with another pair, exchange your results and select a spokesperson for your group.

3 My Son the Fanatic

B Understanding the content

1 a) *Read the first section of the story.*

VIP FILE

Hanif Kureishi was born in England in 1954. His mother is English and his father Pakistani. He has been writing since the 1970s and has had success with *My Beautiful Launderette, The Buddha of Suburbia* and the collection *Love in a Blue Time.*

Hanif Kureishi: My Son the Fanatic

Surreptitiously, the father began going into his son's bedroom. He would sit there for hours, rousing himself only to seek clues. What bewildered him was that Ali was getting tidier. The room, which was usually a tangle of clothes, books, cricket bats and video games, was becoming neat and ordered: spaces began appearing where before
5 there had been only mess.

Initially, Parvez had been pleased: his son was outgrowing his teenage attitudes. But one day, beside the dustbin, Parvez found a torn shopping bag that contained not only old toys but computer disks, videotapes, new books, and fashionable clothes the boy had bought a few months before. Also without explanation, Ali had parted from
10 the English girlfriend who used to come around to the house. His old friends stopped ringing.

For reasons he didn't himself understand, Parvez was unable to bring up the subject of Ali's unusual behaviour. He was aware that he had become slightly afraid of his son, who, between his silences, was developing a sharp tongue. One remark Parvez did
15 make – "You don't play your guitar anymore" – elicited the mysterious but conclusive reply, "There are more important things to be done."

Yet Parvez felt his son's eccentricity as an injustice. He had always been aware of the pitfalls that other men's sons had stumbled into in England. It was for Ali that Parvez worked long hours; he spent a lot of money paying for Ali's education as an
20 accountant. He had bought Ali good suits, all the books he required, and a computer. And now the boy was throwing his possessions out! The TV, video-player and stereo system followed the guitar. Soon the room was practically bare. Even the unhappy walls bore pale marks where Ali's pictures had been removed.

Parvez couldn't sleep; he went more often to the whisky bottle, even when he was at
25 work. He realised it was imperative to discuss the matter with someone sympathetic.

Parvez had been a taxi-driver for twenty years. Half that time he'd worked for the same firm. Like him, most of the other drivers were Punjabis. They preferred to work at night, when the roads were clearer and the money better. They slept during the day, avoiding their wives. They led almost a boy's life together in the cabbies'
30 office, playing cards and setting up practical jokes, exchanging lewd stories, eating takeaways from local balti houses, and discussing politics and their own problems.

But Parvez had been unable to discuss the subject of Ali with his friends. He was too ashamed. And he was afraid, too, that they would blame him for the wrong turning his boy had taken just as he had blamed other fathers whose sons began running around
35 with bad girls, skipping school and joining gangs.

For years, Parvez had boasted to the other men about how Ali excelled in cricket, swimming and football, and what an attentive scholar he was, getting As in most subjects. Was it asking too much for Ali to get a good job, marry the right girl, and start a family? Once this happened, Parvez would be happy. His dreams of doing well in
40 England would have come true. Where had he gone wrong?

One night, sitting in the taxi office on busted chairs with his two closest friends, watching a Sylvester Stallone film, Parvez broke his silence.

"I can't understand it!" he burst out. "Everything is going from his room. And I can't talk to him any more. We were not father and son – we were brothers! Where has he
45 gone? Why is he torturing me?" And Parvez put his head in his hands.

Even as he poured out his account, the men shook their heads and gave one another knowing glances.

"Tell me what is happening!" he demanded.

The reply was almost triumphant. They had guessed something was going wrong.
50 Now it was clear: Ali was taking drugs and selling his possessions to pay for them. That was why his bedroom was being emptied.

---

¹ **surreptitiously** secretly
² **to rouse oneself** to become motivated
² **to bewilder** to confuse
³ **tidy** clean, orderly
³ **tangle** confused mass of things
⁷ **dustbin** large container for rubbish
⁷ **torn** full of holes
⁹ **to part from sb** to leave sb
¹⁵ **to elicit** to provoke
¹⁵ **conclusive** final
¹⁸ **pitfall** dangerous situation
¹⁸ **to stumble** *here:* to get into difficulty by chance
²⁰ **accountant** person who controls the financial accounts of businesses
²³ **pale** hardly noticeable
²⁷ **Punjabi** sb from the province of Punjab, Pakistan
²⁹ **cabby** *(infml)* taxi-driver
³⁰ **lewd** speaking about sex in a rude way
³¹ **takeaway** restaurant where you buy meals to take with you
³¹ **balti** spicy Indian dish served in a wok-like pot
³⁶ **to boast** to talk proudly about one's achievements
³⁶ **to excel** to do extremely well
³⁷ **scholar** student
⁴¹ **busted** *(infml)* broken
⁴³ **to burst out, burst, burst** to speak loudly, suddenly
⁴⁵ **to torture sb** to cause sb extreme pain
⁴⁶ **to pour sth out** *here:* to tell sth eagerly
⁴⁶ **account** report

48

"What must I do, then?"

Parvez's friends instructed him to watch Ali scrupulously and to be severe with him, before the boy went mad, overdosed, or murdered someone.

Parvez staggered out into the early-morning air, terrified that they were right. His boy – the drug-addict killer!

To his relief, he found Bettina sitting in his car.

Usually the last customers of the night were local "brasses", or prostitutes. The taxi-drivers knew them well and often drove them to liaisons. At the end of the girls' night, the men would ferry them home, though sometimes they would join the cabbies for a drinking session in the office. Occasionally, the drivers would go with the girls. "A ride in exchange for a ride," it was called.

Bettina had known Parvez for three years. She lived outside the town and, on the long drives home, during which she sat not in the passenger seat but beside him, Parvez had talked to her about his life and hopes, just as she talked about hers. They saw each other most nights.

He could talk to her about things he'd never be able to discuss with his own wife. Bettina, in turn, always reported on her night's activities. He liked to know where she had been and with whom. Once, he had rescued her from a violent client, and since then they had come to care for each other.

Though Bettina had never met Ali, she heard about the boy continually. That night, when Parvez told Bettina that he suspected Ali was on drugs, to Parvez's relief, she judged neither him nor the boy, but said, "It's all in the eyes." They might be bloodshot; the pupils might be dilated; Ali might look tired. He could be liable to sweats, or sudden mood changes. "OK?"

Parvez began his vigil gratefully. Now that he knew what the problem might be, he felt better. And surely, he figured, things couldn't have gone too far?

He watched each mouthful the boy took. He sat beside him at every opportunity and looked into his eyes. When he could, he took the boy's hand, checked his temperature. If the boy wasn't at home, Parvez was active, looking under the carpet, in Ali's drawers, and behind the empty wardrobe – sniffing, inspecting, probing. He knew what to look for: Bettina had drawn pictures of capsules, syringes, pills, powders, rocks.

Every night, she waited to hear news of what he'd witnessed. After a few days of constant observation, Parvez was able to report that although the boy had given up sports, he seemed healthy. His eyes were clear. He didn't – as Parvez expected he might – flinch guiltily from his father's gaze. In fact, the boy seemed more alert and steady than usual: as well as being sullen, he was very watchful. He returned his father's long looks with more than a hint of criticism, of reproach, even – so much so that Parvez began to feel that it was he who was in the wrong, and not the boy.

"And there's nothing else physically different?" Bettina asked.

"No!" Parvez thought for a moment. "But he is growing a beard."

One night, after sitting with Bettina in an all-night coffee shop, Parvez came home particularly late. Reluctantly, he and Bettina had abandoned the drug theory, for Parvez had found nothing resembling any drug in Ali's room. Besides, Ali wasn't selling his belongings. He threw them out, gave them away, or donated them to charity shops.

Standing in the hall, Parvez heard the boy's alarm clock go off. Parvez hurried into his bedroom, where his wife, still awake, was sewing in bed. He ordered her to sit down and keep quiet, though she had neither stood up nor said a word. As she watched him curiously, he observed his son through the crack of the door.

The boy went into the bathroom to wash. When he returned to his room, Parvez sprang across the hall and set his ear to Ali's door. A muttering sound came from within. Parvez was puzzled but relieved.

Once this clue had been established, Parvez watched him at other times. The boy was praying. Without fail, when he was at home, he prayed five times a day.

Parvez had grown up in Lahore, where all young boys had been taught the Koran. To stop Parvez from falling asleep while he studied, the maulvi had attached a piece of string to the ceiling and tied it to Parvez's hair, so if his head fell forward, he would instantly jerk awake. After this indignity, Parvez had avoided all religions. Not that the

[53] **scrupulously** very carefully
[53] **severe** strict –
[55] **to stagger** to walk unsteadily as if one is going to fall
[56] **drug addict** sb who regularly takes drugs and can't live without them
[59] **liaison** *here:* meeting where one has sex
[61] **ride** *(double meaning)* driving sb in one's car/ having sex
[72] **relief** feeling of happiness when sth bad does not happen
[73] **bloodshot** red as if filled with blood
[74] **pupil** small, black circle in the centre of the eye
[74] **dilated** bigger than normal
[74] **to be liable to sth** *(fml)* to be likely to have sth
[76] **vigil** a purposeful watch
[77] **to figure** to think
[82] **syringe** tube with a needle for injections
[83] **rock** *(sl)* crack cocaine
[87] **to flinch** to avoid
[87] **gaze** a fixed look
[87] **alert** paying full attention
[88] **sullen** unwilling to talk
[89] **reproach** criticism
[94] **reluctantly** unwillingly
[94] **to abandon** to give up
[96] **to donate** to give for free
[96] **charity shop** second-hand shop which sells clothing cheaply to those in need
[100] **crack** narrow opening
[102] **muttering** quiet so that one cannot easily be heard
[105] **without fail** always
[106] **Lahore** capital of the province of Punjab in north-east Pakistan –
[107] *maulvi* Muslim religious teacher
[109] **to jerk awake** to wake up suddenly
[109] **indignity** injury to one's self-respect

3 | My Son the Fanatic

*112 **to rove** to look with the aim of starting a sexual relationship*
*114 **inquisitive** curious*
*114 **oddly** strangely*
*115 **devotions** here: prayers*
*118 **to yearn** to have a strong desire*

l other taxi-drivers had any more respect than he. In fact, they made jokes about the
110 local mullahs walking around with their caps and beards, thinking they could tell people how to live while their eyes roved over the boys and girls in their care.
Parvez described to Bettina what he had discovered. He informed the men in the taxi office. His friends, who had been so inquisitive before, now became oddly silent. They
115 could hardly condemn the boy for his devotions.
 Parvez decided to take a night off and go out with the boy. They could talk things over. He wanted to hear how things were going at college; he wanted to tell him stories about their family in Pakistan. More than anything, he yearned to understand how Ali had discovered the "spiritual dimension", as Bettina called it.
120 To Parvez's surprise, the boy refused to accompany him. He claimed he had an appointment. Parvez had to insist that no appointment could be more important than that of a son with his father.

b) *Now read these statements. Decide whether they are true or false. Quote or paraphrase words from the text that confirm or disprove the ideas in the statement and fill in the right-hand column.* →S11

	True	False	Evidence (1 to 15 words)
Searching his son's bedroom Parvez finds drugs.			
He immediately confronts his son with the evidence.			
Parvez wants his son to become an assimilated Englishman.			
He is afraid of revealing his agony to his cab driver friends.			
When he informs them they tell him that Ali is taking drugs.			
Bettina has been Parvez's girlfriend for three years.			
They have talked about their pasts and the misery each has endured.			
When Parvez tells her about his suspicion she tells him to check his son's eyes.			
Parvez finds that his son has started to look guilty.			
Bettina and he abandon their drug theory.			
Parvez finds out that his son has started to pray regularly.			
Parvez has given up his religion because it makes life easier for him in England.			

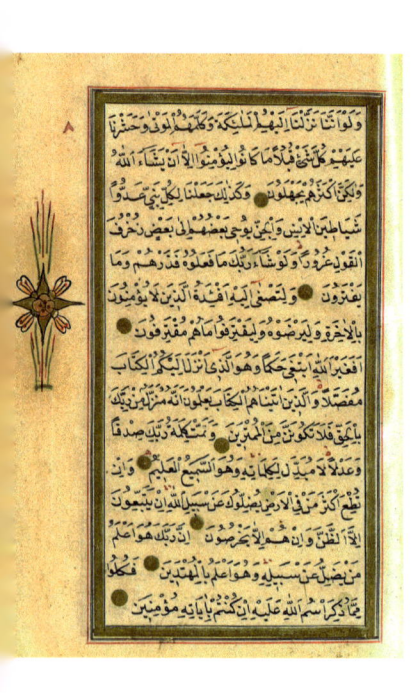

2 a) *Now read the remaining part of the story.*

The next day, Parvez went immediately to the street corner where Bettina stood in the rain wearing high heels, a short skirt, and a long mac, which she would open hopefully at passing cars.

"Get in, get in!" he said.

They drove out across the moors and parked at the spot where, on better days, their view unimpeded for miles except by wild deer and horses, they'd lie back, with their eyes half-closed, saying, "This is the life." This time Parvez was trembling. Bettina put her arms around him.

"What's happened?"

"I've just had the worst experience of my life."

As Bettina rubbed his head Parvez told her that the previous evening, as he and his son had studied the menu, the waiter, whom Parvez knew, brought him his usual whisky-and-water. Parvez was so nervous he had even prepared a question. He was going to ask Ali if he was worried about his imminent exams. But first he loosened his tie, crunched a poppadum, and took a long drink.

Before Parvez could speak, Ali made a face.

"Don't you know it's wrong to drink alcohol?" he had said.

"He spoke to me very harshly," Parvez said to Bettina.

"I was about to castigate the boy for being insolent, but I managed to control myself."

Parvez had explained patiently that for years he had worked more than ten hours a day, had few enjoyments or hobbies, and never gone on holiday. Surely it wasn't a crime to have a drink when he wanted one?

"But it is forbidden," the boy said.

Parvez shrugged. "I know."

"And so is gambling, isn't it?"

"Yes. But surely we are only human?"

Each time Parvez took a drink, the boy winced, or made some kind of fastidious face. This made Parvez drink more quickly. The waiter, wanting to please his friend, brought another glass of whisky. Parvez knew he was getting drunk, but he couldn't stop himself. Ali had a horrible look, full of disgust and censure. It was as if he hated his father.

Halfway through the meal, Parvez suddenly lost his temper and threw a plate on the floor. He felt like ripping the cloth from the table, but the waiters and other customers were staring at him. Yet he wouldn't stand for his own son's telling him the difference between right and wrong. He knew he wasn't a bad man. He had a conscience. There were a few things of which he was ashamed, but on the whole he had lived a decent life.

"When have I had time to be wicked?" he asked Ali.

In a low, monotonous voice, the boy explained that Parvez had not, in fact, lived a good life. He had broken countless rules of the Koran.

"For instance?" Parvez demanded.

Ali didn't need to think. As if he had been waiting for this moment, he asked his father if he didn't relish pork pies?

"Well." Parvez couldn't deny that he loved crispy bacon smothered with mushrooms and mustard and sandwiched between slices of fried bread. In fact, he ate this for breakfast every morning.

Ali then reminded Parvez that he had ordered his wife to cook pork sausages, saying to her. "You're not in the village now. This is England. We have to fit in."

Parvez was so annoyed and perplexed by this attack that he called for more drink.

"The problem is this," the boy said. He leaned across the table. For the first time that night, his eyes were alive. "You are too implicated in Western civilisation."

Parvez burped; he thought he was going to choke. "Implicated!" he said. "But we live here!"

"The Western materialists hate us," Ali said. "Papa, how can you love something which hates you?"

---

[2] **mac** *short for* **mackintosh** raincoat
[6] **unimpeded** unrestricted
[7] **to tremble** to shake a little
[14] **imminent** certain to happen soon
[15] **to crunch** to chew noisily
[15] **poppadum** thin, round, crisp Indian bread
[16] **to make a face** to put on an ugly expression
[19] **to castigate** *(fml)* to criticise severely
[19] **insolent** rude, disrespectful
[25] **to shrug** to move your shoulders up and down to show that you don't care
[26] **gambling** playing games for money
[28] **to wince** to tighten your muscles suddenly as in pain
[28] **fastidious** very critical
[31] **disgust** a strong dislike
[34] **to rip** to pull violently
[35] **to stand for sth** *(infml)* to allow sth to happen
[37] **decent** respectable
[39] **wicked** evil
[44] **to relish** to enjoy a lot
[45] **to smother** to cover thickly
[50] **perplexed** surprised
[52] **implicated** involved
[53] **to burp** to make a noise in one's throat as air comes out of one's stomach
[53] **to choke** to fail to breathe

3 | My Son the Fanatic

58 rowdy noisy, likely to cause trouble
59 to quell to beat down
60 infidel sb without religious beliefs
60 Christer (sl) Christian
61 to rout to defeat completely
61 sink here: place of evil
61 hypocrite sb who pretends to be what he/she is not
61 adulterer sb who is sexually disloyal to a wife or husband
65 jihad holy war by Muslims against non-Muslims in defence of the Islamic faith
70 to urge to make a great effort to persuade
70 to mend one's ways to improve morally
73 to usher to lead
86 to stumble here: to almost fall down
87 to scrape to injure through contact with sth rough
87 to haul oneself up to pull oneself to one's feet with great effort
90 to dislodge to remove
96 usury (fml, old) lending money at an exorbitant rate of interest
107 to give up on sb to stop supporting sb
108 superstitious believing in things that are not real, e.g. magic
109 to stick by sb to continue to try to help sb

"What is the answer, then," Parvez said miserably, "according to you?"
Ali didn't need to think. He addressed his father fluently, as if Parvez were a rowdy crowd which had to be quelled or convinced. The law of Islam would rule the world; the skin of the infidel would burn off again and again; the Jews and Christers would be routed. The West was a sink of hypocrites, adulterers, homosexuals, drug users and prostitutes.

While Ali talked, Parvez looked out the window as if to check that they were still in London.

"My people have taken enough. If the persecution doesn't stop, there will be jihad. I, and millions of others, will gladly give our lives for the cause."

"But why, why?" Parvez said.

"For us, the reward will be in Paradise."

"Paradise!"

Finally, as Parvez's eyes filled with tears, the boy urged him to mend his ways.

"But how would that be possible?" Parvez asked.

"Pray," urged Ali. "Pray beside me."

Parvez paid the bill and ushered his boy out of there as soon as he was able. He couldn't take any more.

Ali sounded as if he'd swallowed someone else's voice.

On the way home, the boy sat in the back of the taxi, as if he were a customer. "What has made you like this?" Parvez asked him, afraid that somehow he was to blame for all this. "Is there a particular event which has influenced you?"

"Living in this country."

"But I love England," Parvez said, watching his boy in the rear view mirror. "They let you do almost anything here."

"That is the problem," Ali replied.

For the first time in years, Parvez couldn't see straight. He knocked the side of the car against a lorry, ripping off the wing mirror. They were lucky not to have been stopped by the police: Parvez would have lost his licence and his job.

Back at the house, as he got out of the car, Parvez stumbled and fell in the road, scraping his hands and ripping his trousers. He managed to haul himself up. The boy didn't even offer him his hand.

Parvez told Bettina he was willing to pray, if that was what the boy wanted – if it would dislodge the pitiless look from his eyes. "But what I object to," he said, "is being told by my own son that I am going to Hell!"

What had finished Parvez off was the boy's saying he was giving up his studies in accounting. When Parvez had asked why, Ali said sarcastically that it was obvious. "Western education cultivates an anti-religious attitude."

And in the world of accountants it was usual to meet women, drink alcohol, and practise usury.

"But it's well-paid work," Parvez argued. "For years you've been preparing!"

Ali said he was going to begin to work in prisons, with poor Muslims who were struggling to maintain their purity in the face of corruption. Finally, at the end of the evening, as Ali went up to bed, he had asked his father why he didn't have a beard, or at least a moustache.

"I feel as if I've lost my son," Parvez told Bettina. "I can't bear to be looked at as if I'm a criminal. I've decided what to do."

"What is it?"

"I'm going to tell him to pick up his prayer mat and get out of my house. It will be the hardest thing I've ever done, but tonight I'm going to do it."

"But you mustn't give up on him," said Bettina. "Many young people fall into cults and superstitious groups. It doesn't mean they'll always feel the same way." She said Parvez had to stick by his boy.

Parvez was persuaded that she was right, even though he didn't feel like giving his son more love when he had hardly been thanked for all he had already given.

For the next two weeks, Parvez tried to endure his son's looks and reproaches. He attempted to make conversation about Ali's beliefs. But if Parvez ventured any criticism, Ali always had a brusque reply. On one occasion, Ali accused Parvez of
115 "grovelling" to the whites; in contrast, he explained, he himself was not "inferior"; there was more to the world than the West, though the West always thought it was best.

"How is it you know that?" Parvez said. "Seeing as you've never left England?"

Ali replied with a look of contempt.

120 One night, having ensured there was no alcohol on his breath, Parvez sat down at the kitchen table with Ali. He hoped Ali would compliment him on the beard he was growing, but Ali didn't appear to notice it.

The previous day, Parvez had been telling Bettina that he thought people in the West sometimes felt inwardly empty and that people needed a philosophy to live by.

125 "Yes," Bettina had said. "That's the answer. You must tell him what your philosophy of life is. Then he will understand that there are other beliefs."

After some fatiguing consideration, Parvez was ready to begin. The boy watched him as if he expected nothing. Haltingly, Parvez said that people had to treat one another with respect, particularly children their parents. This did seem, for a moment,
130 to affect the boy. Heartened, Parvez continued. In his view, this life was all there was, and when you died, you rotted in the earth. "Grass and flowers will grow out of my grave, but something of me will live on."

"How then?"

"In other people. For instance, I will continue – in you."

135 At this the boy appeared a little distressed.

"And in your grandchildren." Parvez added for good measure. "But while I am here on earth I want to make the best of it. And I want you to, as well!"

"What d'you mean by 'make the best of it'?" asked the boy.

"Well," said Parvez. "For a start … you should enjoy yourself. Yes. Enjoy yourself
140 without hurting others."

Ali said enjoyment was "a bottomless pit".

"But I don't mean enjoyment like that," said Parvez. "I mean the beauty of living."

"All over the world our people are oppressed," was the boy's reply.

"I know," Parvez answered, not entirely sure who "our people" were. "But still – life is
145 for living!"

Ali said, "Real morality has existed for hundreds of years. Around the world millions and millions of people share my beliefs. Are you saying you are right and they are all wrong?" And Ali looked at his father with such aggressive confidence that Parvez would say no more.

150 A few evenings later, Bettina was riding in Parvez's car after visiting a client when they passed a boy on the street.

"That's my son," Parvez said, his face set hard. They were on the other side of town, in a poor district, where there were two mosques.

Bettina turned to see. "Slow down, then, slow down!"

155 She said. "He's good-looking. Reminds me of you. But with a more determined face. Please, can't we stop?"

"What for?"

"I'd like to talk to him."

Parvez turned the cab round and pulled up beside the boy.

160 "Coming home?" Parvez asked. "It's quite a way."

The boy shrugged and got into the back seat. Bettina sat in the front. Parvez became aware of Bettina's short skirt, her gaudy rings and iceblue eyeshadow. He became conscious that the smell of her perfume, which he loved, filled the cab. He opened the window.

165 While Parvez drove as fast as he could, Bettina said gently to Ali, "Where have you been?"

"The mosque," he said. "And how are you getting on at college? Are you working hard?"

---

[112] **to endure** to tolerate
[113] **to venture** to dare *(to say sth)*
[115] **grovelling** *(negative)* behaving in an excessively polite way
[119] **contempt** dislike
[127] **fatiguing** tiring
[128] **haltingly** uncertainly, slowly
[128] **to hearten** to encourage
[135] **distressed** upset
[136] **for good measure** to add an extra example
[141] **a bottomless pit** *here:* sth that uses up one's energy
[153] **mosque** *Moschee*
[155] **determined** resolute, firm
[162] **gaudy** colourful in a vulgar way

3 My Son the Fanatic

¹⁷¹ **inadvertently** unintentionally
¹⁷⁷ **fury** uncontrolled anger
¹⁸⁸ **to pace** to walk with regular steps
¹⁸⁹ **to glance** to look quickly
¹⁹² **to pant** to breathe noisily
¹⁹³ **to retaliate** to hit back when sb hurts you

"Who are you to ask me these questions?" Ali said, looking out of the window. Then they hit bad traffic, and the car came to a standstill.
By now, Bettina had inadvertently laid her hand on Parvez's shoulder. She said, "Your father, who is a good man, is very worried about you. You know he loves you more than his own life."
"You say he loves me," the boy said.
"Yes!" said Bettina.
"Then why is he letting a woman like you touch him like that?"
If Bettina looked at the boy in anger, he looked back at her with cold fury.
She said, "What kind of woman am I that I should deserve to be spoken to like that?"
"You know what kind," he said. Then he turned to his father. "Now let me out."
"Never," Parvez replied.
"Don't worry, I'm getting out," Bettina said.
"No, don't!" said Parvez. But even as the car moved forward, she opened the door and threw herself out – she had done this before – and ran away across the road. Parvez stopped and shouted after her several times, but she had gone.
Parvez took Ali back to the house, saying nothing more to him. Ali went straight to his room. Parvez was unable to read the paper, watch television, or even sit down. He kept pouring himself drinks.
At last, he went upstairs and paced up and down outside Ali's room. When, finally, he opened the door, Ali was praying. The boy didn't even glance his way.
Parvez kicked him over. Then he dragged the boy up by the front of his shirt and hit him. The boy fell back. Parvez hit him again. The boy's face was bloody. Parvez was panting; he knew the boy was unreachable, but he struck him none the less. The boy neither covered himself nor retaliated: there was no fear in his eyes. He only said, through his split lip. "So who's the fanatic now?"

From: Hanif Kureishi, *Love in a Blue Time*, 1997

b) *Read these statements and put the letter of the correct answer into the box below.* →S11

1. Parvez picks up Bettina in order to tell her about
   a) the best day of his life.
   b) his son's drinking problem.
   c) his son's criticising him for drinking alcohol.
   d) his having had an accident.

2. When he asks his son why he thinks that he is evil, Ali tells him that
   a) he is having an affair with a prostitute.
   b) he neglects his mother.
   c) he has forced him to adopt British norms and values.
   d) he violates numerous rules of the Koran.

3. During their conversation Ali points out
   a) Western civilisation has always persecuted the Muslims.
   b) there will be a jihad and that he will take part in it.
   c) the West no longer rules the world.
   d) his father loves those that hate him.

4. Ali tells his father that he is giving up his studies in accountancy because
   a) he wants to work with Muslim prisoners.
   b) accountancy is not a well-paid profession.
   c) accountants are often corrupt.
   d) accountancy is not suitable for a Muslim.

5. Telling Bettina about his worries Parvez remarks that he
   a) has started to hate his son.
   b) can't bear to be told that he is a criminal.
   c) doesn't want his son to move out.
   d) thinks he has lost his son.

6. Ali believes that
   a) his father is inferior to white Englishmen.
   b) he himself is superior to the English.
   c) his father has a subserviant attitude towards the English.
   d) his father is a coward.

7. One evening Ali is picked up by his father on his return from
   a) a Mosque.
   b) a secret meeting with Muslim fundamentalists.
   c) his social work in a prison.
   d) a football match between two Muslim teams.

8. During the ride in the taxi Bettina
   a) accuses Ali of not obeying his father.
   b) wonders why he has given up his studies.
   c) assures him of his father's love.
   d) tells him that he must stop antagonising his father.

My Son the Fanatic | 3

9. At home Parvez attacks his son because
   a) he has found out about his relationship with Bettina.
   b) he wants to make his son obey him again.
   c) Ali hates him.
   d) he hates Ali.

1. ☐   2. ☐   3. ☐   4. ☐   5. ☐   6. ☐   7. ☐   8. ☐   9. ☐

C Analysis

1 a) *Re-read the story and note in the space below examples from the text that reveal aspects of your subject's character.* →S7

b) Speaking: [👥/👥👥] *Compare your notes, first with your neighbour, then with the other members of your group. Then agree on the examples and what they reveal. Collect them on a poster and add one characteristic that according to your group captures your subject best. Then put your results up on the wall. When all the groups have finished, do a gallery walk.* →S24

> **TIP**
>
> Divide the class into five groups. The first two groups deal with Ali, the next two groups concentrate on Parvez (the two main characters), the fifth group deals with Bettina

Ali/Parvez/Bettina:

Examples from the text	What each example reveals about his/her character.

> **TIP**
>
> **The gallery walk**
> Go to each exhibition item, listen to each group's speaker and comment on the respective group's findings. If you find fault with anything, be constructive in your criticism i. e. make suggestions for improvements.

c) Writing: *Write a character study of about 200 words on the person you have chosen.* →S7

3 My Son the Fanatic

2 *Divide the story into four sections in class and explain the function of each section.* →S9

Section of story/content	Function

3 *Establish the narrative perspective and examine how it influences the reader's perception of both Ali and Parvez. The example below will help you:* →S8

> Fact: Ali was getting tidier.
> Perspective: It bewildered Parvez.

4 [👥] *Discussion: Discuss with your partner the advantages and disadvantages of the chosen point of view with regard to the characters of Ali and Parvez. Make notes first, then write the results on a separate piece of paper.*

Advantages

_____
_____
_____
_____

Disadvantages

_____
_____
_____
_____

My Son the Fanatic | 3

5 *Analyse the restaurant scene. In doing so, consider the verbal exchanges between father and son as well as their non-verbal behaviour.* →S7

Verbal exchanges:

Father	Son

Analysis of the verbal exchanges

3 My Son the Fanatic

Behaviour:

Father	Son

Analysis of the verbal exchanges

6 Creative writing. Examine the story's ending. How would you answer Ali's question "so who's the fanatic now"? → S12

My Son the Fanatic | 3

D Further activities

1 a) *Listening: Listen to the interview with Ed Husain, a former Muslim extremist. Put the letter of the correct answer in the box below.* →S21

1. The interviewer asks Ed Husain to talk about his …
   a) upbringing.
   b) British identity.
   c) experiences at school.
   d) link to extremist groups.

2. Ed Husain points out that …
   a) the Scots, the Welsh and the Irish all have their own identities.
   b) unlike the British the Americans have a very unclear sense of identity.
   c) Britishness is made up of regional aspects.
   d) Britishness is very hard to define.

3. The interviewee remarks that …
   a) his generation grew up in two different cultures.
   b) his parents refused to integrate into British society.
   c) Britishness was defined to him at school.
   d) the idea of his having a British identity is foolish.

4. Ed Husain speaks about …
   a) the successful interaction between white British children and the children of immigrants.
   b) how the concept of multiculturalism has enriched British society.
   c) the monocultural ghettos that prevent ethnic interaction.
   d) communities that have overcome ethnic separation.

5. The interviewer wonders …
   a) why Ed Husain gave up the idea of becoming an imam.
   b) why he became an extremist.
   c) why he broke with radical Islam.
   d) whether his experiences helped him to find his identity.

6. When Husain first went to mosques he …
   a) found it difficult to relate to the teachings by the imams.
   b) enjoyed the folkloric Islam that was taught in the mosques.
   c) had difficulties in understanding the teaching as it was in Urdu.
   d) was fascinated by an Islam that was village-based.

7. Later on Husain …
   a) was made to attend mosques in which only English was used.
   b) became a follower of traditional orthodox Islam.
   c) came to realise that the English-speaking Muslims were radicals.
   d) was forced by his parents to break with English-speaking Muslims.

1. ☐ 2. ☐ 3. ☐ 4. ☐ 5. ☐ 6. ☐ 7. ☐

b) *Compare the reasons Ed Husain gives for young Muslims becoming extremists with Ali's situation. Note similarities and differences.*

Similarities: _____

_____

_____

Differences: _____

_____

_____

FACT FILE

Ed Husain was born in London, where he went to school. He has lived and travelled in the Middle East and worked for the British Council there. A former founding director of Quilliam, a counter-extremism thinktank, he is the author of the controversial book *The Islamist* (2007). He now lives in New York City.

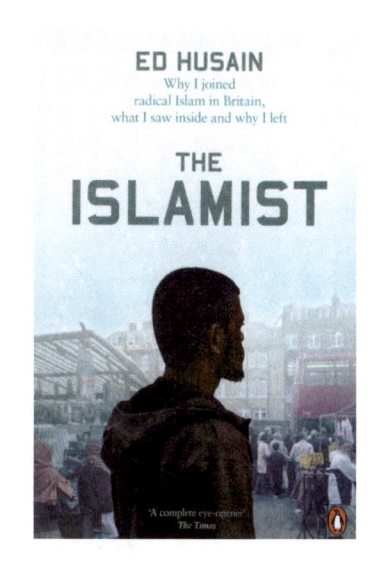

3 | My Son the Fanatic

TIP

Present reasons for your camera work.
Explain why you have chosen a particular type of shot or point of view and the effect you wish to create with it.

USEFUL PHRASES

The camera takes a … shot.

The camera zooms/tilts/pans/tracks/ …

In the foreground/background there is …

The viewer is meant to …

The focus is on a …

This brings us close to/creates a distance between …

This creates a … atmosphere.

8 [👥] *Creative Writing:* Get together in teams of four and write a script for the confrontation scene between Ali and his father in the restaurant. Before you start, look at the screenplay of "The Queen and the PM" on pages 18/19 in *Green Line Oberstufe Niedersachsen*. This will give you an idea of what a screenplay looks like.

Your script should include the following points:
– What the scenery (the inside of the restaurant) should look like.
– How you want to use the camera.
– How Ali and his father should look (clothes, facial expressions) and speak.
– How facial expressions and body language should emphasise what is being said.
– How the waiter and the other customers react when Parvez loses his temper.

In addition, add information about the camera work. Consider angles, points of view and types of shots.
Decide on aspects you want to deal with as a whole team and on those which you will deal with individually.
For this task refer to the special skill on the visual aspects of film that your teacher will give you. It will help you when you write the information about the camera work. →S12

9 [👥] *Debate:* The subject of wearing Islamic headscarves by teachers is extremely controversial. Organise a debate on the following motion (proposal): →S26
Female teachers should be banned from wearing Islamic headscarves at this school.

Group 1: *for*

- Collect arguments for your position.
- Try to anticipate the other side's arguments and prepare possible counter-arguments.
- Decide on how you want to present yourself and your contribution to the debate (aggressive? calm? thoughtful? …).
- When you have prepared all important aspects of your role, decide which two of you will present your position.

Group 2: *against*

- Collect arguments for your position.
- Try to anticipate the other side's arguments and prepare possible counter-arguments.
- Decide on how you want to present yourself and your contribution to the debate (aggressive? calm? thoughtful? …).
- When you have prepared all important aspects of your role, decide which two of you will present your position.

TIP

The legal situation does not make a debate superfluous, although the law can be used in the arguments.

Group 3: *working on an evaluation sheet (approx. 6 students)*

- Get together in teams of two and devise an evaluation sheet to assess the debate.
- Collect assessment criteria (e.g. body language, self-assertiveness, choice of words) and note them down.
- Share your findings with another team, complete your list.
- Repeat this process with yet another team (you are now a group of six).
- Work on a ranking: which criterion is most, which is least important?
- Design an evaluation sheet.
- Don't forget to use practical assessment grades (++;+;o;–;–– or ☺☺/☺/☹/☹☹).
- Appoint one assessor for each speaker.
- After the debate compare your notes and (together) present your results.
- Remember to always make a point of the strengths of each participant in the debate.

Group 4: *chairperson and audience*

- The chairperson moderates the two rounds of exchanges. After the last round the chairperson invites questions and comments from the audience.
- Get together in teams of two or three and prepare questions you want to ask and (depending on your point of view) comments you wish to make. Then share your ideas with another team. Decide whether you want to be matter-of-fact or somewhat polemical.

FACT FILE

The legal situation
Germany
Eight of Germany's 16 states have restrictions on the wearing of the hijab by female teachers, including Lower Saxony. States can ban by state law the wearing of Islamic headscarves by female teachers. It is not regarded as an infringement of the constitutional protection of freedom of religion.
The UK
The house of Lords ruled in 2006 that the banning of Islamic dress in schools was legal as it did not restrict religious freedom. In the same year a teacher was sacked for insisting on wearing the hijab, a face veil.

Chapter 4 The Great Gatsby

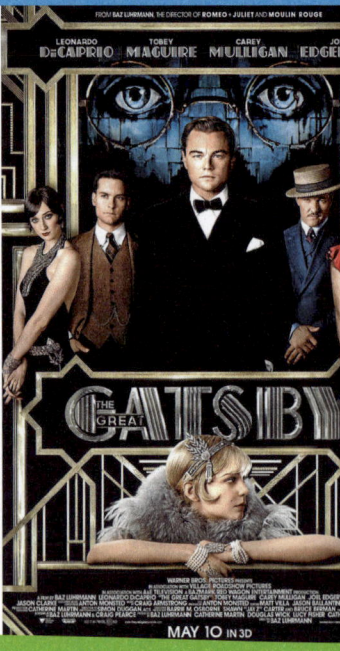

A Introduction

1 a) Pre-reading actvity: The following excerpt is from "The Great Gatsby", the novel that you are going to read. Gatsby is talking to Nick Carraway, his neighbour, who is the narrator of the novel.

[...] "Well, I'm going to tell you something about my life," he interrupted. "I don't want you to get a wrong idea of me from all these stories you hear."
So he was aware of the bizarre accusations that flavored conversations in his halls.
5 "I'll tell you God's truth." His right hand suddenly ordered divine retribution to stand by. "I am the son of some wealthy people in the middle-west - all dead now. I was brought up in America but educated at Oxford because all my ancestors have been educated there for many years. It is a family tradition."
He looked at me sideways – and I knew why Jordan Baker had believed he was
10 lying. He hurried the phrase "educated at Oxford," or swallowed it or choked on it as though it had bothered him before. And with this doubt his whole statement fell to pieces and I wondered if there wasn't something a little sinister about him after all.
"What part of the middle-west?" I inquired casually.
15 "San Francisco."
"I see."
"My family all died and I came into a good deal of money." [...]
"After that I lived like a young rajah in all the capitals of Europe – Paris, Venice, Rome – collecting jewels, chiefly rubies, hunting big game, painting a little,
20 things for myself, and trying to forget something very sad that had happened to me long ago." [...]

⁵ **retribution** deserved punishment for a crime or misdeed
⁶ **to stand by** to support or help
¹⁰ **to choke on sth.** not to be able to breathe because one cannot swallow sth. properly; **rajah** formerly a ruler or prince in India
¹⁹ **ruby** Rubin
¹⁹ **big game** large wild animals

The Great Gatsby | 4

b) *Scan this excerpt for information about Gatsby and make a list of the results.* →S11

_____
_____
_____
_____
_____
_____
_____
_____
_____
_____
_____
_____
_____
_____
_____
_____
_____

c) *Based on this information speculate on the sort of person Gatsby is.*
d) [⚇] **Presentation:** *Now exchange your ideas with a partner. Note where you agree and disagree and present your ideas in class.*

B Understanding the content

The nine chapters of the novel can be divided into five sections. While reading them, do the exercises and tasks on each section.

Chapters I–II →S11

1 a) *Put the letter of the correct answer into the box below.*

1. The I-narrator Nick Carraway goes East, because
    a) he took part in the Great War.
    b) his fiancee lives there.
    c) he wants to learn the bond business.
    d) he goes to college there.

2. Gatsby's house in West Egg is
    a) a Colonial mansion.
    b) an imitation of a French hotel.
    c) a weather beaten bungalow.
    d) a colossal affair that looks like a French town hall.

3. When the narrator describes Tom Buchanan for the first time, he points out
    a) his aggressive and arrogant manner.
    b) his effeminate mannerisms.
    c) his big, hulking body.
    d) his witty ways.

4. When Daisy Buchanan is first introduced to the reader, we get the impression that she is
    a) a woman with many faces.
    b) a foolish and naive person.
    c) a woman dominated by her husband.
    d) a simple woman who enjoys her motherhood.

4 | The Great Gatsby

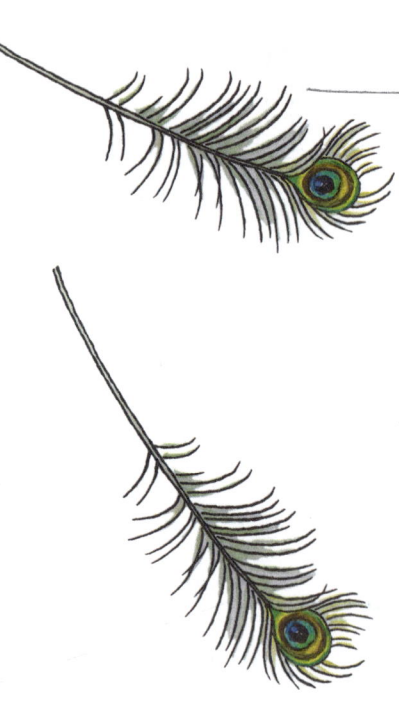

5. Daisy confesses to Nick that she is
   a) very happy in East Egg.
   b) optimistic about the future.
   c) cynical and pessimistic.
   d) in love with another man.

6. Myrtle Wilson, Tom Buchanan's mistress, is married to
   a) a successful car salesman
   b) an underpaid clerk
   c) a rich car dealer
   d) a garage owner

7. Myrtle's sister Catherine tells Nick that Gatsby is said to be
   a) in the "artistic" business
   b) a German millionaire
   c) a cousin of Kaiser Wilhelm
   d) a rich banker

8. Tom Buchanan breaks Myrtle's nose because
   a) she shouts out the name of his wife.
   b) she has another lover.
   c) she speaks ill of Daisy.
   d) he is a violent and sadistic person.

1. ☐ 2. ☐ 3. ☐ 4. ☐ 5. ☐ 6. ☐ 7. ☐ 8. ☐

b) *Speculate on how the plot will unfold. Jot down a few sentences.*

_____
_____
_____
_____
_____

Chapters III–IV →S11

2 a) *Decide whether the statements are true or false. Give evidence from the text to confirm or disprove the point made in each statement and put it in the right-hand column.*

	True	False	Evidence (1 to 15 words)
Nick Carraway smuggles himself into Gatsby's party.			
The party is characterised by a carefree, hilarious atmosphere.			
During his party Gatsby mingles with his guests and is an attentive host.			
Nick enjoys Jordan Baker's company because she is extremely honest.			
When Gatsby and Nick drive to New York, Nick has the impression that Gatsby is an important man.			
During the car ride Gatsby tells Nick that he is from a poor background.			

Furthermore he tells him that he was a highly decorated officer in Montenegro's army during World War I.		
When a policeman stops Gatsby for speeding, he is not given a ticket because he shows him a card from the head of the New York City police.		
Mr Wolfshiem, Gatsby's friend, was once a witness to a murder.		
Carraway learns from Gatsby that Wolfshiem manipulated the outcome of baseball games in 1919.		

b) *What is your impression of Gatsby at this point? What kind of person do you think he is? Write about a 100 words on a separate piece of paper and re-consider what you thought of him after reading the excerpt from the novel.*

Chapter V →S11

3 a) *Read the 10 statements. Determine the correct order and put the numbers in the boxes.*

- ✓ 6 [7] Gatsby shows Daisy and Nick around his house.
- ✓ 9 [9] Mr Klipspringer plays a tune for them on the piano.
- ✓ 2 [1] Nick Carraway invites Daisy for tea at his house.
- ✓ 3 [4] After Daisy arrives Gatsby knocks at Nick's front door.
- ✓ 1 [2] Gatsby offers Nick Carraway a job "on the side".
- ✓ 8 [8] Gatsby receives a mysterious telephone call that he abruptly ends.
- ✓ 4 [3] After a while Gatsby believes that meeting Daisy again was a terrible mistake.
- ✓ 7 [10] After Gatsby has taken Daisy and Nick on a tour of his house, he shows them his garden, the pool and his hydroplane.
- ✓ 10 [5] When Nick leaves Gatsby he notices an expression of confusion on his face.
- ✓ 5 [6] Later Gatsby's face glows with happiness.

b) *Daisy and Gatsby meet for the first time in 5 years. Speculate on how their relationship will develop?*

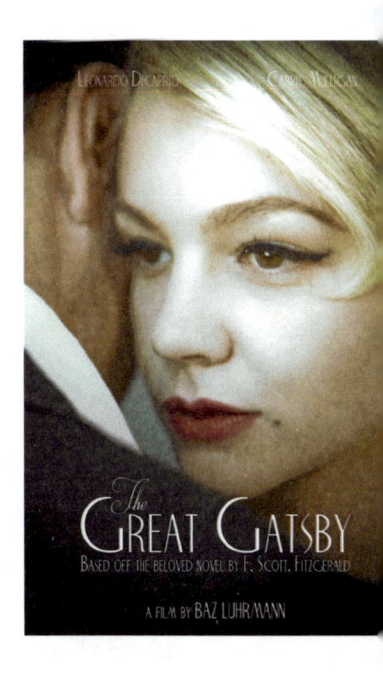

_____
_____
_____
_____
_____
_____
_____
_____

4 The Great Gatsby

Chapters VI–VII → S11

4 a) *Put the letter of the correct answer in the box below.*

1. One of the rumours about Gatsby was that he
   a) owned a big ocean-going yacht.
   b) was in charge of a ring of alcohol smugglers.
   c) had adopted a new name.
   d) lived in a boat that looked like a house.

2. Before becoming Dan Cody's handyman Gatsby had
   a) studied theology at a small Lutheran college.
   b) worked as a janitor for a millionaire.
   c) worked as a clam digger and salmon fisher.
   d) had been unemployed.

3. When Tom and Daisy Buchanan attend Gatsby's party, the atmosphere is
   a) particularly oppressive and unpleasant.
   b) simply hilarious.
   c) aggressive and vulgar.
   d) monotonous and boring.

4. Tom Buchanan suspects that Gatsby is a
   a) gambler.
   b) bootlegger.
   c) foreign agent.
   d) fraud.

5. Suddenly Gatsby no longer hosts lavish parties, because
   a) people have started to shun him.
   b) he has become sick.
   c) Daisy, who regularly sees him, disapproves of these parties.
   d) he has become tired of playing host.

6. Daisy tells Gatsby that she loves him in front of
   a) Jordan Baker.
   b) her husband and Nick.
   c) Jordan Baker and Nick.
   d) her daughter.

7. When the party goes to New York.
   a) Tom Buchanan drives Gatsby's car.
   b) Gatsby takes everyone in his car.
   c) Nick and Jordan Baker drive Tom's coupé.
   d) Daisy drives her husband's coupé.

8. When Tom stops at Wilson's garage to get some gas
   a) Wilson tells him that he and his wife will sell the garage and go south.
   b) Wilson tells him that he has come by some money recently and will go west.
   c) Tom says that he will let Wilson have his coupé.
   d) Tom says that he bought the yellow car he is driving the week before.

9. Inside the suite of the Plaza Hotel
   a) Tom accuses Gatsby of never having been to Oxford.
   b) Gatsby tells Tom that Daisy has never loved him.
   c) Daisy states that she has always and only loved Tom.
   d) Tom tells Daisy to drive back in Gatsby's car.

10. Investigating the hit and run accident, the policeman
    a) finds out that Myrtle Wilson was killed by a car going into New York.
    b) questions Nick Carraway thoroughly.
    c) learns from a Negro that Myrtle Wilson was run over by a yellow car.
    d) suspects that Tom Buchanan knows the driver of the hit and run car.

1. ☐ 2. ☐ 3. ☐ 4. ☐ 5. ☐ 6. ☐ 7. ☐ 8. ☐ 9. ☐ 10. ☐

b) *What important information about Daisy and the Buchanans' relationship becomes clear during the discussion at the kitchen table after the hit and run? Write about 80 words.*

Chapters VIII–IX →S11

5 a) *Decide whether the statements are true or false. In the right-hand column quote or paraphrase words from the text that confirm or disprove the ideas in the statement.*

	True	False	Evidence (1 to 15 words)
From the beginning of his love affair with Daisy Gatsby was insincere to her.			
He led her to believe that he would be able to provide for her.			
Instead of going home at the end of the war Gatsby went to Oxford.			
Leaving Gatsby after breakfast, Nick tells him that he has always disapproved of him.			
When Jordan Baker calls him at the office they agree to meet for lunch.			
George Wilson believes that the driver of the yellow car murdered his wife.			
George Wilson shoots Gatsby at his pool and escapes.			
Wilson's motive for killing Gatsby is jealousy.			
Nick Carraway makes the arrangements for Gatsby's funeral.			
Gatsby's father is informed about his son's death by Nick			
Meyer Wolfshiem tells Nick that he managed Gatsby's rise from rags to riches.			
Hundreds of people attend Gatsby's funeral.			
Tom Buchanan is finally responsible for Gatsby's death.			

b) *Mr. Gatz has a very positive view of his son. On a separate piece of paper present textual evidence for this view and speculate on why this is.*

4 | The Great Gatsby

C Analysis

Chapter I →S7, →S9

p. 5–7/19

1 *Examine how the narrator introduces himself in the first six paragraphs.*
a) *Make notes.*

_____
_____
_____
_____
_____

b) *Write a short answer on a separate piece of paper.*

2 *Point out what we learn about Nick Carraway in chapter 1.*
a) *Fill in the chart below.*

Nick Carraway

Function in the novel: _____

Place of birth: _____

Family background: _____

Main biographical data: _____
_____

Job: _____

Predominant character traits: _____

---

b) *Write a short answer on a separate piece of paper.*

USEFUL PHRASES

hypocrite; infidelity; one-dimensional figure; flirtatious; insubstantial, brittle

3 [👥] *Fill in the character profiles in the charts below with your partner.*

Tom Buchanan	Daisy Buchanan
Place of birth: _____	physical characteristics: _____
Family background: _____	_____
Physical appearance: _____	Personality: _____
_____	_____
Main biographical data: _____	_____
_____	_____
_____	_____
Job: _____	_____
Predominant character traits: _____	_____
_____	_____
_____	_____
_____	_____

The Great Gatsby | 4

Jordan Baker	Gatsby
Physical characteristics: _____	Narrator's opinion: _____
Personality: _____	_____
Special features: _____	_____
_____	_____
_____	_____
_____	_____

4 *Examine the description of Gatsby's house (West Egg) and that of the Buchanans' (East Egg).*

Gatsby's house: _____

_____

The Buchanans' house: _____

_____

USEFUL PHRASES

pompousness; pretentiousness; fake

5 *Describe the Buchanans' way of life and their relationship to each other.*

6 *Comment on Nick Carraway's reaction when leaving the Buchanans'.*

Chapter II →S5, →S7

7 **Setting and Characters – the Wilsons.** *Use a separate piece of paper for the results.*
   a) *Describe the main characteristics of the valley of ashes. In doing so, consider also its location and function.*
   b) *Characterise George Wilson. In what way is he a typical inhabitant of the valley of ashes?*
   c) *Work out the main characteristics of Myrtle Wilson by examining the following words and phrases. Then fill in the character profile below.*

USEFUL PHRASES

symbolic landscape; wasteland

> sensuous, vitality (28 25,27)
> I'm going to give you this dress as soon as I'm through with it (38/21)
> swept into the kitchen, implying a dozen chefs awaited her orders there" (34/39)
> he had on a dress suit and patent leather shoes" (38/10)
> walking through her husband as if he were a ghost" (28/29)
> I knew right away I made a mistake" (36/16)

Myrtle Wilson

predominant quality: _____

main motive: _____

behaviour in New York: _____

real status: _____

relationship to her husband: _____

USEFUL PHRASES

to be contemptuous of sb

   d) *Take a look again at the character profile of Tom Buchanan (cf. chapter I). Which other character traits can you add?*

_____

8 [👥] *List the new information about Gatsby you have learned in this chapter.*

_____

4 The Great Gatsby

USEFUL PHRASES

a claim to unbiased objectivity vs. tendency to romanticise

9 [👥] *Determine Nick's role in this chapter. Consider his description of New York's 5th Avenue as well as his observation "I was within and without, simultaneously enchanted and repelled." (38/3–5)*

Chapters III–IV →S5, →S7, →S12

10 *Gatsby and his parties.*

a) *Point out the main features of Gatsby's parties by filling in the chart below.*

Gatsby's parties
General character: _____
Setting: _____
Guests: _____
Behaviour: _____
Social contacts: _____
Relationship to the host: _____

USEFUL PHRASES

to keep to o.s.; aloof, aloofness

b) *Describe Gatsby's role as host? What is remarkable about it?*

_____
_____
_____
_____

c) *Summarise what we learn about Gatsby in chapter III.*

negative: _____

mysterious: _____

positive: _____

TIP

Don't forget to stay in character. The points made about the guests and the reporter's questions will give you an idea of the sort of person they are.

d) [👥👥👥] **Role play:** *Work in teams of four.*
One of you is a society reporter for The New York Post. The others are party guests. The society reporter interviews the party guests about what it's like to be invited to one of Jay Gatsby's famous parties. Be prepared to act out the interviews in front of the class.
Look at the information about the four people in this role play. Add some more points **for your character**.

Reporter:	**Guest 1:**
Who is this Gatsby? Reason for party? Choice of people on guest list	young, uninvited, absolutely adores the parties, lots to eat and above all drink, other guests interesting

Guest 2:	**Guest 3:**
old money (East Egg), certainly no expenses spared, many other old friends and acquaintances there, dislikes the vulgarity, lots of uninvited guests	wonders about the host's absence, sometimes things get out of hand, too much alcohol, too many people seeking partners

The Great Gatsby | 4

11 *Gatsby and Daisy – their past.* Do this task on a separate piece of paper. →S7
  a) Examine in detail what Gatsby reveals about himself while driving with Nick to New York. In doing so, consider why Gatsby reveals this information and what he seeks to achieve by it.
  b) Contrast this information with Nick's assessment of Gatsby, his meeting Meyer Wolfshiem and Jordan Baker's relevation about Gatsby's relationship with Daisy.

Chapter V →S5; S7

12 *The reunion of Gatsby and Daisy.*
  a) Analyse Gatsby's mental and emotional state prior to and during Daisy's visit.
  _____
  _____
  _____

  b) Examine Nick's comments on the happiness of the newly united lovers.
  _____
  _____
  _____

  c) Explain why Gatsby is so eager to show Daisy his house and his shirts.
  _____
  _____
  _____

  d) In this context discuss the role material riches play in the relationship between Daisy and Gatsby.
  _____
  _____
  _____

> **TIP**
>
> 12d) can be done with a partner.

Chapters VI–VII →S5, →S9, →S12

13 *Aspects of Gatsby's past.*
  a) Point out who James Gatz was.
  _____
  _____
  _____

  b) Examine the role Dan Cody played in Gatsby's life.
  _____
  _____
  _____
  _____

  c) Describe the essential elements of Gatsby's dreams.
  _____
  _____
  _____
  _____

4 The Great Gatsby

TIP

Work on tasks 14, 15 and 16a) in teams of four.

14 [👥] *Divide chapter VII into five parts. Find a heading for each and note what happens.*

Pages	Section	What happens
part 1:		
part 2:		
part 3:		
part 4:		
part 4:		

15 [👥] *Analyse the scene of the confrontation between Gatsby and Tom Buchanan inside the Plaza Hotel. Why does Tom win the fight? Fill in the chart below.*

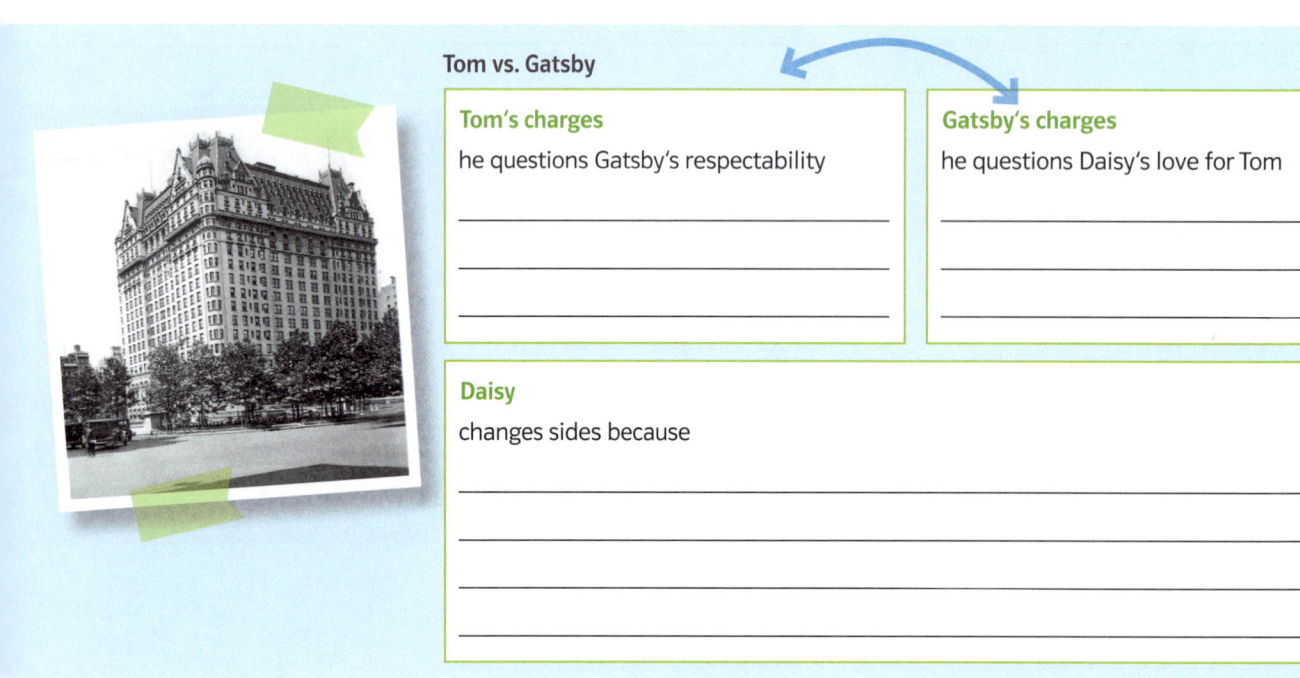

Tom vs. Gatsby

Tom's charges
he questions Gatsby's respectability
_____
_____
_____

Gatsby's charges
he questions Daisy's love for Tom
_____
_____
_____

Daisy
changes sides because
_____
_____
_____
_____

16 a) [👥] *The hit and run accident. Explain how Myrtle's death comes about. In doing so, consider how the information about the accident is provided by the narrator.*

_____
_____
_____
_____

The Great Gatsby | 4

b) Creative writing:
The following interrogation of Daisy and Tom Buchanan takes place on the day after the hit and run.
Fill in the answers and write down Daisy's thoughts and feelings
→ S5, → S7, → S9

TIP

When doing the task keep in mind that Daisy drove Gatsby's car and that there were no witnesses who could identify her.
Interior monologue: use the simple present, short, even elliptic sentences and exclamations

Interrogation

Police Officer: Mrs. Buchanan, how did you get home when you left the Plaza Hotel?
Daisy: _____

Police Officer: Why didn't you ride home with your husband?
Daisy: _____

Police Officer: Did Mr. Gatsby drive the car himself or did you drive it?
Daisy: _____

Police Officer: Mr. Buchanan, how closely did you follow the car that your wife was going home in?
Tom: _____

Police Officer: Can you tell me who was driving the car?
Tom: _____

Police Officer: Did you notice anything when you were approaching Mr Wilson's garage?
Tom: _____

Police Officer: Do you have any idea who might have run over Mrs Wilson?
Tom: _____

Police Officer: OK! Thank you very much.

Interior monologue (Daisy)

Oh, my God! He suspects me! What shall I say?

_____

4 | The Great Gatsby

Chapters VIII–IX

> **TIP**
>
> Use the **think-pair-share** method when dealing with task 18. Work on tasks 19 and 20 with a partner.

17 Examine Gatsby's retrospective narration about his past relationship with Daisy. In doing so, consider why he fell in love with her and whether he was sincere in courting her.

18 Comment on Nick's final evaluation of Gatsby: "They're a rotten crowd. You're worth the whole damn bunch put together." (**145**/13–14) Consider also Nick's assessment from the very beginning of the novel.

19 Review the relationship between the following characters – Jay Gatsby, Daisy and Tom Buchanan, Myrtle and George Wilson and Nick Carraway – by drawing a graph that illustrates the way these characters are connected to each other.

---

the main characters and their relationships

---

20 a) Gatsby's death. Speculate on why Wilson kills Gatsby and afterwards shoots himself.
  b) Explain why virtually no one came to Gatsby's funeral. Consider in particular Wolfshiem and Daisy.

21 [👥] **Presentation:** Form four groups, and revisit some of the main characters. Each group deals with one character. Check your previous notes and examine the pages mentioned below. Prepare a presentation on your character and decide who in your group will give that presentation. Your presentation should include a critical evaluation, e.g. your personal view of the given person's character. →**S22**

Group 1: Nick: In addition to your previous analyses of chapters 1 and 2 pay attention to the following pages: 51, 58–60; 90–94; 164–165.	**Group 2: Daisy** Apart from your findings in chapters 1 and 2 consult the following pages for further information: 73–77; 126–128; 141–142
Group 3: Tom Reconsider the character profile of Tom in chapters 1 and 2. Add further information by re-examining the fight between Gatsby and Tom as depicted in chapter 7.	**Group 4: Jordan** Complete your character profile by studying the following pages: 58–59; 78; 166.

The Great Gatsby 4

D Further activities

1. [👥👥👥] **Presentation: Gatsby and the American Dream.** →S5, →S7, →S22, →23
   a) Examine the following quotes from the novel and work out the stages of Gatsby's rise from rags to riches.

   "His parents were shiftless and unsuccessful farm people." (**96**/4–5)
   "Of course we was broke up when he run off from home. … He knew he had a big future in front of him." (**161**/21–23)
   "Jimmy was bound to get ahead. He always had some resolves like this…" (**162**/19–20)
   "He invented just the sort of Jay Gatsby that a seventeen-year-old boy would be likely to invent, and to this conception he was faithful to the end." (**96**/10–12)
   He despised "the janitor's work with which he was to pay his way through" college. (**97**/10)
   The millionaire Dan Cody left him with a "singularly appropriate education." (**99**/1–2)
   "However glorious might be his future as Jay Gatsby, he was at present a penniless young man without a past…" (**140**/23–24)
   "He had committed himself to the following of a grail." (**141**/10–11)
   "He did extraordinary well in the war." (**142**/13)
   "He came back from France…and made a miserable but irresistible journey to Louisville on the last of his army pay." […] "He was penniless now." (**143**–**144**/31–1)
   "I raised him up out of nothing, right out of the gutter." (**160**/10)
   "He rose up to his position in the East." (**157**/21–22)

   b) Consider this advice Benjamin Franklin gave to a young businessman (tradesman):

   > **The Way to Wealth, if you desire it, is as plain as the Way to Market. It depends chiefly on two Words, INDUSTRY and FRUGALITY: i.e. Waste neither Time nor Money, but make the best Use of both. He that gets all he can honestly, and saves all he gets will certainly become RICH.**

   Compare this advice to Gatsby's resolves for his own life. In doing so, you should point out how Gatsby perverted the American ideal of the self-made man.
   c) Point out how Gatsby wants to realise his teenage dreams.
   d) Considering his resolves, evaluate the fact that he rejects a formal education as a means to success.
   e) Briefly explain the role that Mr. Wolfshiem plays in Gatsby's life.
   f) Discuss whether Gatsby's biography is a story of corruption or the result of a tragic love affair. The aim of the discussion is to come to a conclusion backed up with evidence from the novel.

2. [👥👥] **Creative writing:** Write an article on Gatsby to be published in a celebrity magazine. First of all note down your own ideas for such an article, then compare your notes with a partner, before you write the article together. Possible topics for such an article could be: Gatsby's mansion and his cars; Gatsby's parties; The rumours about Gatsby, Gatsby's funeral.

TIP

A good way of dealing with the task in 1 is to get together in groups of four. Prepare a presentation, if possible, a powerpoint presentation. If more than one group is dealing with this topic, exchange results and arrange for a joint presentation.

FACT FILE

Benjamin Franklin (1705–1790), one of the Founding Fathers of the United States, was a strong believer in moral values and virtues as a basis for society.

USEFUL PHRASES

list of virtues; ideal of self-improvement; to rise, to get ahead; penniless; relentless ambition; greedy materialism; distorted/perverted ideas of the American Dream

TIP

Celebrity magazine articles usually contain these features:
- celebrity depicted positively
- use of emotionally-charged adjectives
- celebrity portrayed as "human", not superman/superwoman
- celebrity's hobbies, preferences, a few harmless weaknesses

3 Mediation: Your class is co-operating with an American high school on a project about the way Fitzgerald's novel has been received in the USA and Germany.
Your research comes up with this article. Write a mail of about 200 words to your partner school in America containing the main points the author makes and a short opinion on the article. →S33

Wenn der Leser ins Schwitzen kommt

F. Scott Fitzgeralds Roman „Der große Gatsby"
Jay Gatsby gehört zu den Figuren, die größer sind als die Romane, denen sie entspringen. Längst lebt er auf eigene Rechnung und hat seinen Schöpfer hinter sich
5 gelassen. Francis Scott Fitzgerald, jung, berühmt und ein berüchtigter Trinker, wurde nur 44 Jahre alt. Der Star der Literaturszene der Zwanzigerjahre endete verschuldet und verbittert in Los Angeles. 1940 lag ein abgezehrter Leichnam im Sarg.

10 „Der große Gatsby" erschien 1925, als die USA noch im wirtschaftlichen Boom steckte, mitten im Jazz. Es ist die Geschichte einer fatalen Wiederbegegnung. Ein armer Kerl, der sein Mädchen
15 an einen reichen Mann verloren hat, arbeitet sich empor und kommt mit Hilfe dunkler Geschäfte an ein Vermögen. Sein Anwesen auf Long Island, das viele Geld, die rauschenden Partys, die Gats-
20 by gibt, dienen nur dazu, die verlorene Geliebte anzulocken. Wie viele große Romanfiguren ist Gatsby ein reichlich unwahrscheinlicher Charakter. Welcher Mann von solch blendendem Äußeren
25 und mit solchem Talent zum Geldverdienen träumt Nacht für Nacht den Traum von der Rückgewinnung einer entschwundenen Liebe? Doch der Roman spielt virtuos auf der Klaviatur
30 arm/reich, treu/untreu, und der flüssige, elegante Stil, in dem das vorgetragen wird, erlaubt, dass man Gatsbys melancholische Obsession dennoch für bare Münze nimmt.
35 Zwei Beispiele für den literarischen Rang des Romans: Am entscheidenden Tag, dem Tag des Verhängnisses, ist es derart heiß, dass der Leser in Verfolgung des Geschehens selbst ins Schwit-
40 zen kommt. Ein Glutschwall nach dem anderen dringt durch die Fenster, lastet auf den Figuren und lockert das Korsett der Sitten. Scott Fitzgerald wird hier zum Meister eines brütenden Him-
45 mels, aufgeweichter Asphaltstraßen und dampfender, alkoholisierter Körper. Zur Katastrophe kommt es unten den Riesenaugen des Dr. Eckleburg, dem Plakat eines Augenarztes in einem
50 verwahrlosten, aschfarbenen Gelände zwischen New York und Long Island. Die metergroßen Augen wachen gottgleich über einer Schutthalde. Ihnen entgeht nichts. Der Himmel über dem
55 Roman ist leer, kein Gott straft die reichen Schufte, ihr Gewissen peinigt sie nicht. Aber die bebrillten Augen von T.J. Eckleburg haben alles gesehen.
Gatsby wurde dreimal verfilmt, die Fassung von 1975 mit Robert Redford ist
60 noch im Gedächtnis. Der ist zwar nicht die ideale Verkörperung des Jay Gatsby – ihm fehlt die abgründige Seite. Aber das Drehbuch ist erstklassig; die übrigen Figuren sind gut besetzt. Und Eck-
65 leburg bohrt einem mit seinem Blick noch in den Rücken, nachdem man das Kino verlassen hat. Wer aber Fitzgeralds Gatsby mit seiner romantischen Liebe hinter sich lassen möchte, wer sich für
70 den Leichnam mit den faltigen Händen interessiert, der sollte einfach weiterlesen: seinen „Knacks" und vor allem die Briefe, die er mit seiner Frau Zelda gewechselt hat.
75

*Sibylle Lewitschscharoff,
Süddeutsche Zeitung 2004*

The Great Gatsby | 4

4 Geographical allusions: East and West

a) *Examine the following contexts in which Nick describes the Midwest that he has left and the East that he is leaving. Evaluate these contexts.*

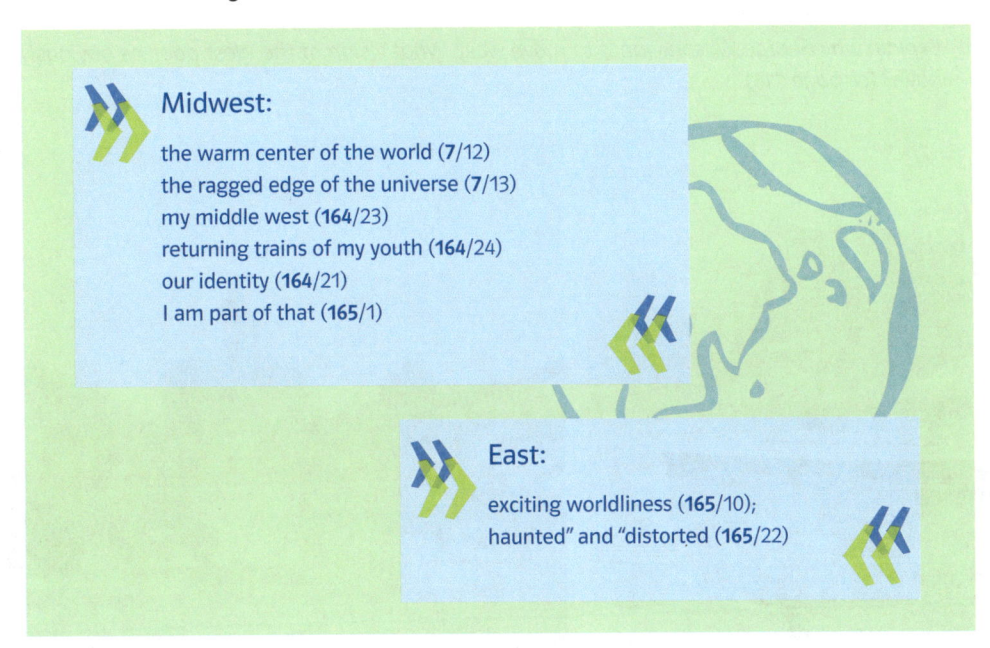

Midwest:
- the warm center of the world (**7**/12)
- the ragged edge of the universe (**7**/13)
- my middle west (**164**/23)
- returning trains of my youth (**164**/24)
- our identity (**164**/21)
- I am part of that (**165**/1)

East:
- exciting worldliness (**165**/10);
- "haunted" and "distorted" (**165**/22)

TIP

A good way of dealing with these tasks is to get together in groups of four. Prepare a presentation, if possible, a power point presentation. If more than one group is dealing with this topic, exchange results and arrange for a joint presentation.

Evaluation: Midwest

_____
_____
_____
_____
_____
_____
_____
_____

Evaluation: The East

_____
_____
_____
_____
_____
_____
_____

USEFUL PHRASES

staid, orderly; idyllic; homeliness

4 The Great Gatsby

TIP

When you present your findings contrast Nick's Midwest with that of Dan Cody and George Wilson.

b) **Discussion:** Bearing in mind that Nick feels disgusted with the East at the end, does his return to the Midwest signal a retreat into a past that no longer exists? Discuss.
c) Collect and evaluate all information about Dan Cody (cf. pages 91, 95–99). Find out who Cody was and what role he played for Gatsby.
d) Explain why George Wilson wants to move west. What vision of the West does he obviously have? (cf. page 118)

5 a) Examine all contexts in which the advertisement with the eyes of Dr. Eckleburg occurs and determine their meaning by filling in the grid below.

	context	impression
page 27		
page 117		
page 150		

USEFUL PHRASES

billboard; to foreshadow; doom; to keep vigil; monstrosity

b) Summarise the function of the eyes of Dr. Eckleburg throughout the novel.

The Great Gatsby | 4

6 *Listening:* The text that you are going to listen to is a letter by Maxwell Perkins who was Fitzgerald's editor at the publishing company Charles Scribner's.
You will listen to the text twice. →S21

a) *After the first listening put the letter of the correct statement in the box.*

1. Maxwell Perkins says about the choice of narrative perspective that it
   a) undercuts any attempt at irony.
   b) enables the reader to view the characters from a distance.
   c) puts the characters on a higher level.
   d) enables the reader to feel the strangeness of human circumstances.

2. The editor finds fault with the portrayal of Gatsby, calling it
   a) less palpable than that of the others.
   b) artistically misconstrued.
   c) somewhat vague.
   d) a mistake.

3. He suggests that Fitzgerald
   a) adds one or two distinct physical characteristics.
   b) does away with the "old sport" phrase.
   c) makes him more vivid so that the reader would know him if he met him on the street.
   d) makes him physically less attractive.

4. He also suggests that Fitzgerald
   a) makes Gatsby's career less mysterious.
   b) explicitly describes the sources of Gatsby's wealth.
   c) re-writes the end of the novel.
   d) should provide some sort of hint that would suggest an explanation of Gatsby's wealth.

1. ☐   2. ☐   3. ☐   4. ☐

b) *After listening a second time do the following tasks.*

1. Point out the aspects that the writer of the letter criticises in Fitzgerald's novel.

   _____
   _____
   _____
   _____

2. [👥] *Comment on these aspects either by supporting the writer or by refuting his criticism. Whatever your response is you are expected to back it up with well-reasoned arguments of your own and with examples from the novel.*

> **TIP**
>
> First of all make notes of your own ideas, then compare these with your partner's notes, before completing the task together.

Chapter 5 *Romeo and Juliet*

A Shakespeare for starters

A play about first love, at the end of which both of the lovers are dead – that is *Romeo and Juliet*, one of the most famous stories in world literature. We want you to enjoy meeting these timeless characters, experience their problems and understand the reasons for the tragedy. In another play – Willy Russell's drama *Educating Rita* – the main character is so amazed at what she experiences in a drama production that she says: "It's fun, tragedy, isn't it?"
"But how can this be fun?" you may ask. Classic dramas of world literature are constantly being heard and watched by and performed for new audiences in new cultural contexts.
So look forward to understanding what the play is about and giving meaning to single words, phrases, scenes, acts, even the entire play. Your active participation in staging scenes, adapting parts of the play for our time, and finding new solutions to ancient conflicts is called for.
The selection of scenes from the play *Romeo and Juliet* deals with a large variety of topics: first love, teenage love, unconditional love; commitment to family, friends, lovers and spouses; problems in the relationship between parents and their adolescent children; the vicious circle of violence; responsibility.
All these topics are equally significant and relevant to young people in the 21st century.

TIP

You will find basic information on Shakespeare himself, his works and his language in **Green Line Oberstufe Niedersachsen**, Topic 16. Always remember that there is more than one correct interpretation of Shakespeare's plays. Everybody has the right to his/her own interpretation of scenes and even whole plays. Everybody has the right to an active approach when dealing with a Shakespeare play. Shakespeare does **not** only have to be endured passively from a seat in the stalls!

1 *With the help of the plot outline provided by your teacher match the characters to the descriptions given below.*

Juliet Capulet • Lord and Lady Capulet • Tybalt • Nurse • Romeo Montague • Lord and Lady Montague • Benvolio • Escales Prince of Verona • Mercutio • Paris • Friar Lawrence

1. Franciscan monk living on his own _____

2. Young man deeply in love _____

3. Parents of an adorable young girl _____

4. Hot-blooded adversary to all Montagues _____

5. Juliet's nanny and friend _____

6. Adorable young girl deeply in love _____

7. Head of the state of Verona _____

Romeo and Juliet | 5

8. Romeo's friend, relative of Escales _____
9. Romeo's parents _____
10. Benevolent friend of Romeo's _____
11. Hopeful suitor to Juliet _____

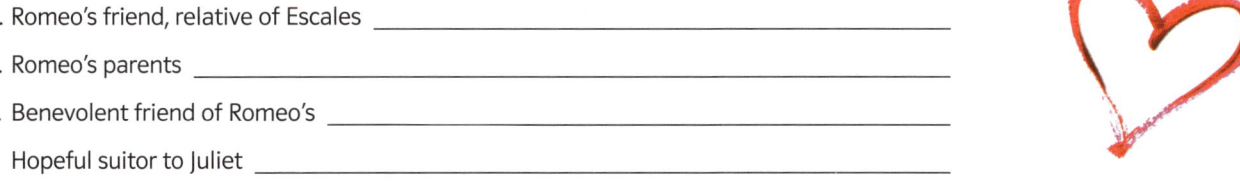

2 [👥] *Get together with a partner, choose a line and speak it out loud together. To find its rhythm, it might help if you link hands and make a "see-saw" movement. Describe what you feel is special about your line or what the line may tell you.*

Romeo	O heavy lightness, serious vanity,	
	Misshapen chaos of well-seeming forms,	I, 1, 169 ff.
Juliet	Parting is such sweet sorrow,	II, 2, 184
Juliet	My only love sprung from my only hate!	I, 5, 137
Friar Lawrende	Virtue itself turns vice, being misapplied,	
	And vice sometime by action dignified.	II, 3, 21 f.
Romeo	He jests at scars that never felt a wound.	II, 2, 1
Romeo	O, I am fortune's fool.	III, 1, 127
Mercutio	They have made worms' meat of me.	III, 1, 97
Juliet	O serpent heart, hid with a flow'ring face!	III, 2, 73
Juliet	My bounty is as boundless as the sea	
	My love as deep;	II, 2, 133 f.
Capulet	Death lies on her like an untimely frost	
	Upon the sweetest flower of all the field	IV, 5, 28
Mercutio	Ask for me tomorrow, and you shall find me a grave man.	III, 1, 89
Lady Capulet	I would the fool were married to her grave.	III, 5, 140
Juliet	O bid me leap, rather than marry Paris,	
	From off the battlements of any tower,	
	Or walk in thievish ways, or bid me lurk	
	Where serpents are; chain me with roaring bears,	
	Or hide me nightly in a charnel-house,	
	O'ercovered quite with dead men's rattling bones, …	IV, 1, 77–82
Nurse	O woe! O woeful, woeful, woeful day!	
	Most lamentable day, most woeful day	
	That ever, ever, I did yet behold!	
	O day, O day, O day, O hateful day!	
	Never was seen so black a day as this.	
	O woeful day, O woeful day!	IV, 5, 49–54

TIP

Rhythm and metre of Shakespeare's writing
One of the fundamental insights into Shakespeare's language is its regular rhythm or beat which is very helpful for the understanding of his plays. The main metre of Shakespeare's writing was a regular rhythm of five units of an unstressed and stressed word, called an iamb. This unit is quite similar to a single heart beat (dee-dum). If you want to imitate Shakespeare's rhythm, try to write lines with five regular stresses, e.g.: dee-dum / dee-dum / dee-dum / dee-dum / dee-dum.

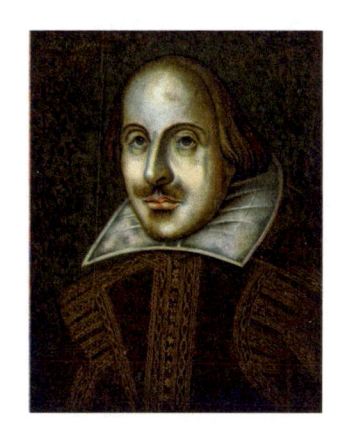

How to start enjoying Shakespeare's texts – basic exercises

1. Get together in a circle and read the text aloud "in a round" everyone reading one word only.
2. Read the text again. Now everyone reads to the next punctuation mark.
3. Now read line by line while those who do not read tap the metre with their hands.
4. Walk around the room speaking one line at a time and at the end of it make a sharp 90 degree turn.
5. Do it again but now turn at every punctuation mark and turn at full stops.
6. The next time only turn when everyone individually feels the end of a sense unit.
7. Finally, from where you are recite the whole passage in whatever way you think right. You may sing, whisper, shout or do whatever you believe to be appropriate.

5 Romeo and Juliet

B Selected extracts and assignments

1 The prologue (Themes and plot)

First focus

TIP

Working with the texts
To help you understand them better, always read the texts both silently and aloud.
When you are doing the assignments in **First focus**, mark in the text important passages or keywords you will need for the solutions.

1 a) *Read the text below and state briefly what the situation in Verona is (lines 1–4).*
_____
_____

b) *Describe what lines 5–8 anticipate and the significance of this situation.*
_____
_____

c) *Identify the driving force of this tragedy as given in lines 9–12.*
_____

2 *Explain the function of the chorus with regard to the plot, the themes and the audience's expectations.*

Plot	Themes	Audience

3 *The prologue is a good example of a regular rhythm in Shakespeare's verse writing.* Mark the text, making five stresses per line and read it out aloud. →S6
Start like this: <u>Two</u> <u>house</u>holds <u>both</u> <u>a</u>like in <u>dig</u>nity, …

Second focus

The following exercises enable you to physically discover the movement of the language before you think hard about its meaning. This connection to the physical voice will help you with the process of understanding..

TIP

Shakespeare did not write his texts to be learned by heart, he wrote them to be performed on stage so you should get used to reading them aloud.
In **Second focus** you have the opportunity to try out some of the of approaches in the **Basic exercises** on page 81.

4 a) *Follow the first Basic exercise from page 81*
b) *Follow Basic exercises 4 and 5 from page 81.*

5 *In some productions the Prince speaks the chorus. Prepare his appearance on stage. Repeat Task 4b), but turn only when you feel the end of a sense unit.*

6 *Add your own interpretation of this scene, using one or more of these modes of expression: singing, whispering, shouting or whatever you feel appropriate.* →S10, →S26

[1] **alike in dignity** of equal social standing
[2] **grudge** anger
[3] **fatal loins … foes** born by old enemies
[4] **star-crossed** under bad influence of the stars
[5] **take their life** are born
[6] **misadventured piteous overthrows** unfortunate events
[7] **strife** quarrel
[8] **fearful passage** tragic developments
[9] **nought** nothing
[10] **toil** labour, hard work

Chorus Two households, both alike in dignity[1],
In fair Verona (where we lay our scene),
From ancient grudge[2] break to new mutiny,
Where civil blood makes civil hands unclean.
From forth the fatal loins of these two foes[3]   5
A pair of star-crossed[4] lovers take their life[5];
Whose misadventured piteous overthrows[6]
Doth with their death bury their parents' strife[7].
The fearful passage[8] of their death-marked love,
And the continuance of their parents' rage,   10
Which but their children's end nought[9] could remove,
Is now the two hours' traffic of our stage;
The which if you with patient ears attend,
What here shall miss, our toil[10] shall strive to mend.

The prologue, 1–14

Romeo and Juliet | 5

2 Re-enacting a vendetta (Organised violence)

First focus

1 *Sampson and Gregory, two Capulet servingmen, start another quarrel with Abram and another Montague servingman. Read the text and outline the main developments of their exchanges in keywords.* →S13

Development
Line 37: _____
Line 42: _____
Line 46: _____
Line 55: _____
Line 58: _____
Line 61: _____

TIP

When you are doing the assignments in **First focus**, mark in the text important passages or keywords you will need for the solutions.

2 *Justify the Prince's decision to punish breaking the peace with the death penalty.*

_____
_____
_____
_____
_____

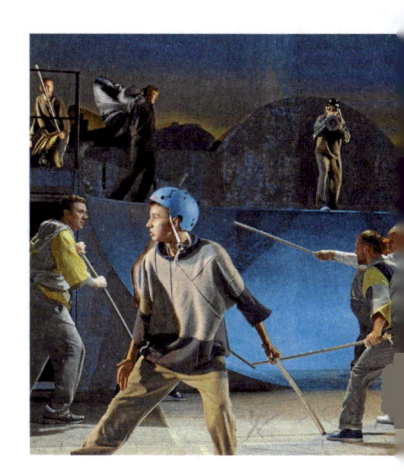

3 [👥] ***Discussion:*** *Discuss possible reactions of the Montagues and Capulets to this decision.* →S26

_____
_____
_____
_____
_____

Second focus

4 [👥] *Shakespeare's language can sometimes be quite strong and offensive, reflecting the taste of his time. The words below are all taken from "Romeo and Juliet".*

1		2		3	
rank	dull	love-devouring	wolvish-ravening	slave	drunkard
reeky	foul	ill-divining	ill-beseeming	ape	knave
rotten	hideous	tallow-faced	self-willed	villain	vice
vain	peevish	tempest-tossed	death-marked	rat-catcher	serpent
vicious	pernicious	savage wild	unlooked-for	rogue	man of wax
wanton	pestilent	life-weary	dog-named	harlotry	worm
bawdy		dove feathered		crutch	

TIP

Let the sound of the insult be the criterion for your choice.
You can look up the meaning of the words you have chosen later in a monolingual and/or a bilingual dictionary. After the exercise, you and your "opponent" tell each other the meaning of the insults you have just hurled at each other.

Create your favourite insult by choosing one word from each column and learn it by heart:

You _____ _____ _____

One group of you is the Capulets and the other the Montagues.
Position yourselves in two lines each facing an "opponent". Now throw your insults at them.
(Remember it is just a game!) →S3

5 Romeo and Juliet

5 Now create three more stinging insults with the words from the list. Look up what they mean.

1. _____ _____ _____
2. _____ _____ _____
3. _____ _____ _____

6 *Vocabulary:* Create a word bank for the term "hate".

Gregory	Draw thy tool, here comes of the house of Montagues. *(Enter two other* SERVINGMEN, *one being* ABRAM*)*	
Sampson	My naked weapon is out. Quarrel, I will back thee.	
Gregory	How, turn thy back and run?	30
Sampson	Fear me not.	
Gregory	No, marry[1], I fear thee!	
Sampson	Let us take the law of our sides, let them begin.	
Gregory	I will frown as I pass by, and let them take it as they list.	
Sampson	Nay, as they dare. I will bite my thumb[2] at them, which is disgrace to them if they bear it.	35
Abram	Do you bite your thumb at us, sir[3].	
Sampson	I do bite my thumb, sir.	
Abram	Do you bite your thumb at us, sir?	
Sampson	*(Aside to Gregory)* Is the law of our side if I say ay[4]?	40
Gregory	*(Aside to Sampson)* No.	
Sampson	No, sir, I do not bite my thumb at you, sir, but I bite my thumb, sir.	
Gregory	Do you quarrel, sir?	
Abram	Quarrel, sir? No, sir.	45
Sampson	But if you do, sir, I am for you. I serve as good a man as you.	
Abram	No better.	
Sampson	Well, sir. *(Enter* BENVOLIO*)*	
Gregory	*(Aside to Sampson)* Say 'better', here comes one of my master's kinsmen.	50
Sampson	Yes, better, sir.	
Abram	You lie.	
Sampson	Draw, if you be men. Gregory, remember thy washing[5] blow. *(They fight.)*	
Benvolio	Part, fools! Put up your swords, you know not what you do. *[Beats down their swords]* *(Enter* TYBALT*)*	55
Tybalt	What, art thou drawn among these heartless hinds[6]? Turn thee, Benvolio[7], look upon thy death.	
Benvolio	I do but keep the peace. Put up thy sword, Or manage it to part these men with me.	60
Tybalt	What, drawn and talk of peace? I hate the word, As I hate hell, all Montagues, and thee. Have at thee, coward. *(They fight.)* […]	I, 1, 28 – 63
Prince	Rebellious subjects, enemies to peace, Profaners of this neighbour-stained steel – Will they not hear? What ho! you men, you beasts, […] Throw your mistempered weapons to the ground And hear the sentence of your moved prince. Three civil brawls, bred of an airy word, By thee, old Capulet, and Montague Have thrice disturbed the quiet of our streets […] If ever you disturb our streets again, Your lives shall pay the forfeit of the peace.	80

I, 1, 72 – 88 95 |

[1] **marry** *(arch)* term to express surprise
[2] **bite my thumb** rude gesture usually shown in Italy
[3] **sir** insult when used repeatedly
[4] **ay** yes
[5] **washing** slashing
[6] **heartless hinds** hind = female deer; heart = pun on hart, the male deer; *(here)* fighting without the master present
[7] **Benvolio** a telling name of Latin origin meaning "good will"

Romeo and Juliet 5

3 The tragic lover

First focus

1. **Pre-reading:** The play starts with serious fighting, yet it is also about the consequences that arise from a new love. Follow the instructions on the worksheet your teacher will give you. →S3

2. Read the excerpt and mark the expressions that denote Romeo's mental state. On a separate sheet of paper describe his state in modern English. →S13

3. Choose two examples from the oxymora in lines 167–174 and explain the atmosphere they help to create. →S10

4. **Writing:** How does Romeo define the state of being in love (lines 176 ff.)? Refer to the "Terms of love" in Task 1 to support your point. Write on a separate sheet of paper.

Second focus

5. Working with lines 176–186 only, first rehearse the text following the exercises of reading aloud (cf. Basic exercises 4–6 on page 81). You are all Romeos and walk through the room. When you meet someone you greet the person with a passage of your choice from the text. Take care to use appropriate intonation and body language.

> **TIP**
>
> An oxymoron uses two incompatible opposites to express a new thought; here they are used to show Romeo's confusion.

Benvolio	Good morrow, cousin.
Romeo	Is the day so young?
Benvolio	But new struck nine.
Romeo	Ay me, sad hours seem long.
	Was that my father that went hence so fast?
Benvolio	It was. What sadness lengthens Romeo's hours?
Romeo	Not having that, which, having, makes them short. 155
Benvolio	In love?
Romeo	Out –
Benvolio	Of love?
Romeo	Out of her favour where I am in love.
Benvolio	Alas that Love, so gentle in his view, 160
	Should be so tyrannous and rough in proof!
Romeo	Alas that Love, whose view is muffled still[1],
	Should, without eyes, see pathways to his will!
	Where shall we dine? O me! what fray[2] was here?
	Yet tell me not, for I have heard it all: 165
	Here's much to do with hate, but more with love:
	Why then, O brawling love, O loving hate,
	O any thing of nothing first create!
	O heavy lightness, serious vanity[3],
	Misshapen[4] chaos of well-seeming forms, 170
	Feather of lead, bright smoke, cold fire, sick health,
	Still-waking sleep, that is not what it is!
	This love feel I, that feel no love in this.
	Dost thou[5] not laugh?
Benvolio	No, coz[6], I rather weep.
Romeo	Good heart, at what?
Benvolio	At thy good heart's oppression. 175
Romeo	Why, such is love's transgression:
	Griefs of mine own lie heavy in my breast,
	Which thou wilt propagate[7] to have it pressed
	With more of thine; this love that thou hast shown
	Doth add more grief to too much of mine own. 180
	Love is a smoke made with the fume[8] of sighs,
	Being purged, a fire sparkling in lovers' eyes,
	Being vexed, a sea nourished with loving tears.
	What is it else? a madness most discreet,
	A choking gall[9], and a preserving sweet. 185
	Farewell, my coz.

I, 1, 151–186

[1] **muffled still** always covered
[2] **fray** irritation
[3] **vanity** *(here)* being unimportant
[4] **misshapen** unnatural shape
[5] **dost thou** do you
[6] **coz** cousin
[7] **to propagate** to increase; to make heavier
[8] **fume** *(here)* breath
[9] **gall** *(here)* bitter poison

5 Romeo and Juliet

4 Party time (The lovers meet)

First focus

Part A

1 *Mark phrases and note keywords next to them that describe Romeo in this part of the scene (lines 43–52).* →S4

2 *Explain the reasons why Tybalt cannot kill Romeo at the party (lines 64–72).*

_____

_____

3 [👥] ***Discussion:*** *Compare the way Lord Capulet deals with the "gatecrashers" and the behaviour of the Montagues to what happens at similar parties in the modern world. Take down your keywords and defend your position in a discussion.* →S26

_____

_____

_____

Part B

4 *What do Romeo and Juliet say to each other when they first meet (still disguised in masques)? Mark their words and on a separate sheet of paper outline what happens in modern English.*

5 *Continue the description of Romeo's character from Extract 3, Task 2. Mark keywords in the text before you write.* →S7

6 *Analyse the language of Tybalt, Capulet and the young lovers. Find futher expressions like the examples and then summarise the different types of language used by completing the first line of the table.* →S10

Tybalt	Capulet	Romeo and Juliet
expressions of _____	expressions of _____	expressions of _____
Line 53: rapier	Line 64: content thee	Line 93: this holy shrine
Line 54: slave		
Line 58:		

Second focus (Parts A and B)

7 [👥] *For a new movie production a trailer highlighting this conflict has to be created. In groups of four, each member takes on one of the figures in these extracts. Choose for your character one striking sentence/statement central to the scene. Write down your line and rehearse your mini scene.* →S12

8 [👥] ***Podium discussion:*** *"The notion of love at first sight is an illusion!" Discuss this statement also referring to the ideas uttered in the text (cf. Romeo ll.51f. and 102; Juliet ll. 107 and 109).* →S26

▪ **In the meantime:** Capulet gives Paris his consent to marry his daughter Juliet. He plans a great party. By mistake the Montague boys hear about the party and decide to go. Romeo does not want to go and his friends laugh about him as a hopeless dreamer. Finally Romeo decides to go and encounters a gorgeous girl (cf. plot outline, Act 1, ll. 10–12).

Romeo and Juliet 5

Part A

Romeo O she doth teach the torches to burn bright!
It seems she hangs upon the cheek of night
As a rich jewel in an Ethiop's[1] ear –
Beauty too rich for use, for earth too dear:
So shows a snowy dove trooping with crows,
As yonder lady o'er her fellows shows.
The measure[2] done, I'll watch her place of stand,
And touching hers, make blessèd my rude hand.
Did my heart love till now? forswear it, sight!
For I ne'er saw true beauty till this night.

Tybalt This, by his voice, should be a Montague.
Fetch me my rapier, boy.   *(Exit Page)*
   What dares the slave
Come hither, covered with an antic face[3],
To fleer[4] and scorn at our solemnity[5]?
Now by the stock and honour of my kin,
To strike him dead I hold it not a sin.

Capulet Why, how now, kinsman, wherefore storm you so?

Tybalt Uncle, this is a Montague, our foe:
A villain that is hither come in spite,
To scorn at our solemnity this night.

Capulet Young Romeo is it?

Tybalt   'Tis he, that villain Romeo.

Capulet Content thee, gentle coz, let him alone,
'A bears him like a portly[6] gentleman;
And to say truth, Verona brags of him
To be a virtuous and well-governed youth.
I would not for the wealth of all this town
Here in my house do him disparagement[7];
Therefore be patient, take no note of him;
It is my will, the which if thou respect,
Show a fair presence, and put off these frowns,
An ill-beseeming semblance[8] for a feast.

Tybalt It fits when such a villain is a guest:
I'll not endure him.

Capulet   He shall be endured.   I, 5, 43–75

[1] **Ethiop's** word used for black African
[2] **measure** *(here)* dance
[3] **antic face** very eleborate mask
[4] **to fleer** to laugh at
[5] **solemnity** *(here)* festivity
[6] **portly** *(arch)* impressive, dignified
[7] **disparagement** to belittle, disrespect
[8] **semblance** behaviour

Part B

Romeo *(To Juliet)* If I profane[9] with my unworthiest hand
This holy shrine, the gentle sin is this,
My lips, two blushing pilgrims, ready stand
To smooth that rough touch with a tender kiss.

Juliet Good pilgrim[10], you do wrong your hand too much,
Which mannerly devotion shows in this,
For saints have hands that pilgrims' hands do touch,
And palm to palm is holy palmers'[11] kiss.

Romeo Have not saints lips, and holy palmers too?

Juliet Ay, pilgrim, lips that they must use in prayer.

Romeo O then, dear saint, let lips do what hands do:
They pray, grant thou, lest faith turn to despair.

Juliet Saints do not move, though grant for prayers' sake.

Romeo Then move not while my prayer's effect I take.
Thus from my lips, by thine, my sin is purged.   *(Kissing her.)*

Juliet Then have my lips the sin that they have took.

Romeo Sin from my lips? O trespass[12] sweetly urged!
Give me my sin again.   *(Kissing her again.)*

Juliet   You kiss by th'book[13].   I, 5, 92–109

[9] **to profane** to show contempt for what is sacred, desecreate
[10] **pilgrim** traveller to a religious site
[11] **palmers** pilgrim carrying palm leaves
[12] **tresspass** *(here)* sin
[13] **by th'book** like an expert *(or: learned from theory)*

5 Romeo and Juliet

5 Romeo confesses his love

First focus

1 *Choose three ideas that illustrate Romeo's joy at seeing Juliet at the upstairs window (lines 1–32).*

1. _____ 2. _____ 3. _____

2 *Select three expressions Romeo uses to show his feelings for Juliet which you find especially appealing. Explain how Juliet might have reacted had she heard them. This task can be continued with Task 4.*

Expression	Line	Reaction

3 a) *Trace Juliet's line of argumentation about the significance of a name.* →S26

Line	Text	Significance
l. 38		
l. 43		
l. 47		

b) *Do you think Juliet's suggestion that Romeo should change his name could lead to a solution of the problem?*

_____
_____
_____

Second focus

4 [👥] *With your partner, act out the exchange of compliments you chose in Task 2.*

5 *This is one of the most famous dialogues in world drama. Despite the fact that their thoughts coincide, the two lovers do not speak directly to one another (they can't see each other due to the darkness) but address their words to the audience. Rehearse this scene in the now familiar way (cf. **Basic exercises** on page 81) thus creating your own version of the scene. Follow steps a) and b).*

a) *Practise your speech individually (as Romeos and Juliets) with the aim of expressing your emotions towards the person you love convincingly.* →S22

b) [👥] *In a second step perform your part or the entire scene with a partner.*

> **TIP**
>
> Experiment with different emotions.
> How do you conceive Romeo to be – hesitant, pragmatic, reserved? How does Juliet react? In a shy way or overwhelmed by her love? The text gives you a wide range of possibilities.

Romeo and Juliet

■ **In the meantime:** The party is over and Mercutio has made fun of Romeo who to him is not able to enjoy love. All the friends have left and Romeo is walking in the garden when he sees his new love Juliet at the window (cf. plot outline, Act II. 1–10).

Romeo	*(Romeo advances.)*
	He jests at scars that never felt a wound.
	But soft, what light through yonder[1] window breaks?
	It is the east, and Juliet is the sun.
	Arise, fair sun, and kill the envious moon,
	Who is already sick and pale with grief 5
	That thou, her maid, art far more fair than she.
	Be not her maid, since she is envious;
	Her vestal livery[2] is but sick and green[3],
	And none but fools do wear it; cast it off.
	(Juliet appears aloft as at a window.)
	It is my lady, O it is my love: 10
	O that she knew she were!
	She speaks, yet she says nothing; what of that?
	Her eye discourses[4], I will answer it.
	I am too bold, 'tis not to me she speaks:
	Two of the fairest stars in all the heaven, 15
	Having some business, do entreat her eyes
	To twinkle in their spheres[5] till they return.
	What if her eyes were there, they in her head?
	The brightness of her cheek would shame those stars,
	As daylight doth a lamp; her eyes in heaven
	Would through the airy region stream so bright 20
	That birds would sing and think it were not night.
	See how she leans her cheek upon her hand!
	O that I were a glove upon that hand,
	That I might touch that cheek!
Juliet	Ay me!
Romeo	*(Aside)* She speaks. 25
	O speak again, bright angel, for thou art
	As glorious to this night, being o'er my head,
	As is a wingèd messenger[6] of heaven
	Unto the white-upturnèd[7] wond'ring eyes
	Of mortals[8] that fall back to gaze on him, 30
	When he bestrides[9] the lazy puffing clouds,
	And sails upon the bosom of the air.
Juliet	O Romeo, Romeo, wherefore[10] art thou Romeo?
	Deny[11] thy father and refuse thy name;
	Or if thou wilt not, be but sworn my love, 35
	And I'll no longer be a Capulet.
Romeo	*(Aside)* Shall I hear more, or shall I speak at this?
Juliet	'Tis but thy name that is my enemy;
	Thou art thyself,[12] though not a Montague.
	What's Montague? It is nor hand nor foot, 40
	Nor arm nor face, nor any other part
	Belonging to a man. O be some other name!
	What's in a name? That which we call a rose
	By any other word would smell as sweet;
	So Romeo would, were he not Romeo called, 45
	Retain that dear perfection which he owes[13]
	Without that title. Romeo, doff[14] thy name,
	And for thy name, which is no part of thee,
	Take all myself
Romeo	I take thee at thy word:
	Call me but love, and I'll be new baptised; 50
	Henceforth[15] I never will be Romeo. II, 2, 1–51

[1] **yonder** *(old use)* over there
[2] **vestal livery** virginal uniform *(here)* reference to the moon as Diana the goddess of virginity
[3] **sick and green** supposed indications of an illness of virgins
[4] **discourse** talks
[5] **spheres** the planets were believed to circle the earth on crystal paths *(the spheres)*
[6] **winged messenger** messenger with wings *(i.e. an angel)*
[7] **white upturned** wide open eyes in amazement
[8] **mortals** humans
[9] **to bestride** to get on to
[10] **wherefore** why
[11] **to deny** to say sth is not true
[12] **thyself** yourself
[13] **owes** *(here)* owns
[14] **to doff** *(s)* to give up
[15] **henceforth** as from now

5 | Romeo and Juliet

6 Juliet's answer (A first characterisation)

First focus

1 *Read the text and mark the arguments Juliet uses to convince Romeo that her love is "infinite" (line 135). Find evidence that she is first apprehensive and later sure of her emotions.* →S9

Apprehensive	Line	Emotionally sure	Line

2 *Examine the tone of her speech by referring back to your results in Task 1 above. Mark keywords in the speech and analyse the development of her emotions on a separate sheet of paper.* →S10

3 a) *Discuss whether or not their conversation is acceptable among your friends when discussing matters of love.*

_____
_____

b) *In a second step think about different times and places in which such an exchange about a loving relationship would not be acceptable.*

_____
_____

Second focus

4 Think – pair – share:
a) *Select three pieces of music to accompany this scene in a school production.*

1. _____ 2. _____ 3. _____

b) [👥] **Discussion:** Discuss which of your choices you reckon to be most suitable.
c) **Presentation:** Present your idea to the course highlighting why the melody and the lyrics support the emotions of the protagonists at this particular point. →S22
d) [👥] **Discussion:** In a pyramid discussion decide on the winner of this contest. →S26

Juliet	Thou knowest the mask of night is on my face, 85
	Else would a maiden blush bepaint my cheek
	For that which thou hast heard me speak tonight.
	Fain¹ would I dwell on form, fain, fain deny
	What I have spoke, but farewell compliment.
	Dost thou love me? I know thou wilt say 'Ay'; 90
	And I will take thy word; yet if thou swear'st,
	Thou mayst prove false: at lovers' perjuries²
	They say Jove³ laughs. O gentle Romeo,
	If thou dost⁴ love, pronounce it faithfully;
	Or if thou think'st⁵ I am too quickly won, 95
	I'll frown and be perverse⁶, and say thee nay,
	So thou wilt woo, but else not for the world.
	In truth, fair Montague, I am too fond⁷,
	And therefore thou mayst⁸ think my behaviour light⁹:
	But trust me, gentleman, I'll prove more true 100
	Than those that have more coying to be strange¹⁰.
	I should have been more strange, I must confess,
	But that thou overheard'st¹¹, ere I was ware¹²,
	My true-love passion; therefore pardon me,
	And not impute¹³ this yielding to light love¹⁴, 105
	Which the dark night hath so discoverèd. […]

¹ **fain** with pleasure
² **perjuries** lies in court
³ **Jove** Jupiter, the god of oaths
⁴ **thou dost** you do
⁵ **thou think'st** you think
⁶ **perverse** knowingly showing wrong behaviour
⁷ **fond** *(here)* foolish
⁸ **thou mayst** you may
⁹ **light** *(here)* loose, of low moral standard
¹⁰ **coying to be strange** cleverness to appear distant
¹¹ **thou overheard'st** that you may have overheard
¹² **ere I was ware** before I was aware of it
¹³ **to impute** to ascribe
¹⁴ **light love** false emotions, *(cf. KV6: "casual love")*

Romeo and Juliet 5

Juliet	[...] Although I joy in thee,
	I have no joy of this contract[15] tonight,
	It is too rash, too unadvised, too sudden,
	Too like the lightning, which doth cease to be
	Ere one can say 'It lightens'. Sweet, good night:
	This bud of love, by summer's ripening breath,
	May prove a beauteous flower when next we meet.
	Good night, good night! as sweet repose and rest
	Come to thy heart as that within my breast.
Romeo	O wilt thou leave me so unsatisfied?
Juliet	What satisfaction canst thou have tonight?
Romeo	Th'exchange of thy love's faithful vow for mine
Juliet	I gave thee mine before thou didst request it;
	And yet I would it were to give again.
Romeo	Wouldst thou withdraw it? for what purpose, love?
Juliet	But to be frank[16] and give it thee again,
	And yet I wish but for the thing I have:
	My bounty[17] is as boundless as the sea,
	My love as deep; the more I give to thee
	The more I have, for both are infinite.

II, 2, 85–135

[15] **contract** agreement between two people
[16] **frank** open, honest
[17] **bounty** sth given in large quantities

7 The wedding (The Friar's responsibility)

First focus

1 *Mark in the text what ideas Romeo, Juliet and the Friar have with regard to the marriage.*
a) *Complete the table.* →S13

Romeo	Juliet	Friar Lawrence
____	____	____
____	____	____
____	____	____
____	____	____

b) *Now summarise your results in modern English.*

_____
_____
_____
_____

2 *Friar Lawrence gives advice for a happy marriage. Which images does he use to make Romeo and Juliet understand? Write them down and express them in modern English.* →S10

Line	Image	Modern English
ll. 9 f.		
ll. 11 f.		
l. 15		

5 Romeo and Juliet

TIP

Here are some ideas:
- the reconciliation of the families
- the stubbornness of parents
- his role as a spiritual advisor

3 *Writing:* By performing the ceremony without parental consent, Friar Lawrence is breaking church rules. He has to defend his decision in writing. Prepare his justification in note form here. Then write his well-structured defence on a separate sheet of paper. →S9

_____
_____
_____
_____

4 [👥] [👥👥] **Kompetenzaufgabe:** *Getting married in Verona at the turn of the 16th century meant a girl became the property of her husband as well as of his family. Devotion and unconditional loyalty towards them were expected (and often unquestioned) codes of conduct.*

a) *Juliet (aged 13) and Romeo (just a little older) get married one day after their first meeting at the masque. In pairs or groups (of up to four people) agree on three do's and don'ts for both Romeo and Juliet to sustain a successful relationship / partnership / friendship.*

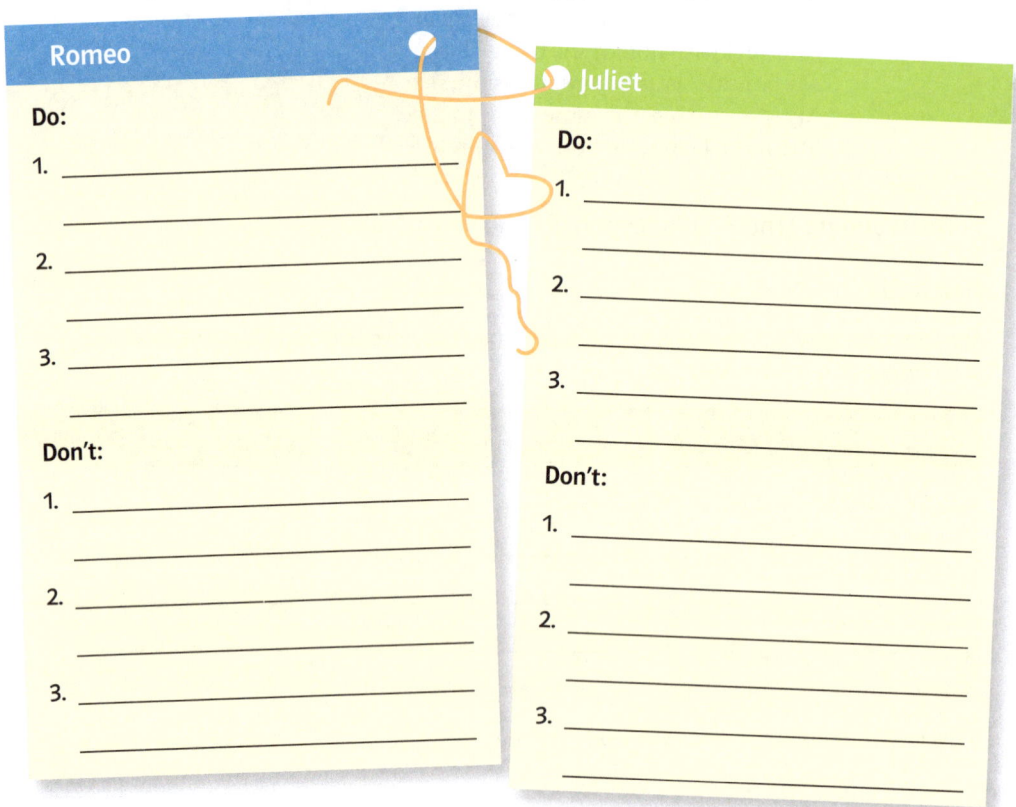

Romeo	Juliet
Do:	**Do:**
1. _____	1. _____
2. _____	2. _____
3. _____	3. _____
Don't:	**Don't:**
1. _____	1. _____
2. _____	2. _____
3. _____	3. _____

TIP

You could publish your findings in a **survey** entitled "How to make your relationship work". Maybe you could put the results in your school magazine, on your school homepage or in the Abitur yearbook.

b) *Presentation: Fill in the list above and / or design a poster with your advice. Present your ideas to your course and back them up by giving adequate justification on why you have included each idea. (If you want to add more suggestions, feel free to do so.)*

c) *Now turn your attention towards a similar situation today. Two adolescents (of your age) intend to get married next month. Which do's and don'ts would you offer them?*

Bridegroom	
Do:	**Don't:**
1. _____	1. _____
2. _____	2. _____
3. _____	3. _____

Bride

Do:
1. _____
_____
2. _____
_____
3. _____
_____

Don't:
1. _____
_____
2. _____
_____
3. _____
_____

d) **Presentation:** Fill in the list above and/or design a poster with your advice. Present your ideas to your course and back them up by giving adequate justification on why you have included each idea. (If you want to add more suggestions, feel free to do so.)

e) [👥👥👥] In your course review all the ideas presented in a)–d). Discuss which ideas you consider helpful guidelines for the future. Say what values were the basis for your choice.

f) [👥👥👥] In your course agree upon the three most valuable suggestions. Follow this procedure:
 – All the girls in the course do so for the suggestions for 1. girls, 2. boys.
 – All the boys in the course do so for the suggestions for 1. boys, 2. girls.
 – The entire course finally compiles the "ultimate" list of advice.

Second focus

5 [👥👥👥] In groups of three, review the definitions you wrote on the sheet used for Task 1 on page 85. Which quotation from your list in Task 1a (page 91) fits your definitions of the "terms of love" best. Rehearse and perform this exchange. Choose from these options: a) a contemporary, very modern theatre production, b) a classical theatre production, c) a trailer for a movie production, d) a personal exchange with a person you love.

■ **In the meantime:** Gathering plants, Friar Lawrence reflects about the fact that many helpful things can also carry dangers. Romeo appears and tells him that he has fallen in love with Juliet. He asks the Friar to marry them. Hoping for an end to the feud the Friar promises help. Juliet sends the Nurse to the Montague boys to find out about the details of the wedding. The Nurse returns to the excited Juliet with the news that Romeo will marry her at the Friar's the same afternoon (cf. plot outline, Act ll. 11–14).

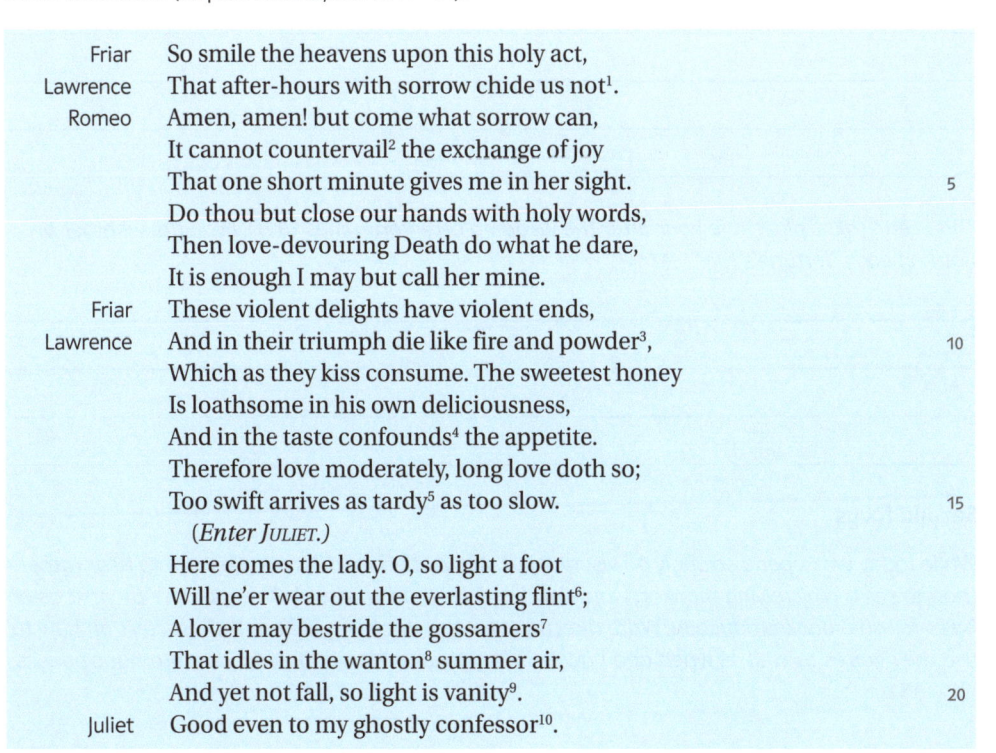

TIP

Clear a space in the classroom for your presentations and place the sheets with the definitions around the room.

Friar Lawrence	So smile the heavens upon this holy act, That after-hours with sorrow chide us not[1].	
Romeo	Amen, amen! but come what sorrow can, It cannot countervail[2] the exchange of joy That one short minute gives me in her sight. Do thou but close our hands with holy words, Then love-devouring Death do what he dare, It is enough I may but call her mine.	5
Friar Lawrence	These violent delights have violent ends, And in their triumph die like fire and powder[3], Which as they kiss consume. The sweetest honey Is loathsome in his own deliciousness, And in the taste confounds[4] the appetite. Therefore love moderately, long love doth so; Too swift arrives as tardy[5] as too slow. *(Enter Juliet.)* Here comes the lady. O, so light a foot Will ne'er wear out the everlasting flint[6]; A lover may bestride the gossamers[7] That idles in the wanton[8] summer air, And yet not fall, so light is vanity[9].	10

15

20 |
| Juliet | Good even to my ghostly confessor[10]. | |

[1] **that after-hours ... not** so that later we are not punished with sadness
[2] **to countervail** to outweigh
[3] **powder** *(here)* gunpowder
[4] **to confound** to confuse *(here)* spoil
[5] **tardy** late, ineffective
[6] **flint** hard stone
[7] **to bestride the gossmers** to walk on the fine threads of spiders
[8] **wanton** *(trad)* behaving in an immoral way
[9] **vanity** *(here)* love's pleasures
[10] **ghostly confessor** spiritual consultant

5 Romeo and Juliet

Friar Lawrence	Romeo shall thank thee, daughter, for us both.
	(Romeo kisses Juliet.)
Juliet	As much to him, else is his thanks too much.
	(Juliet returns his kiss.)
Romeo	Ah, Juliet, if the measure of thy joy
	Be heaped like mine, and that thy skill be more 25
	To blazon[11] it, then sweeten with thy breath
	This neighbour air, and let rich music's tongue
	Unfold the imagined happiness that both
	Receive in either by this dear encounter.
Juliet	Conceit[12], more rich in matter than in words, 30
	Brags[13] of his substance, not of ornament;
	They are but beggars that can count their worth,
	But my true love is grown to such excess
	I cannot sum up sum of half my wealth.
Friar Lawrence	Come, come with me, and we will make short work, 35
	For by your leaves, you shall not stay alone
	Till Holy Church incorporate two in one[14].
	II, 6, 1–37

[11] **to blazon** to make news widely known
[12] **conceit** pride in yourself
[13] **to brag** to talk too proudly
[14] **till Holy Church … one** church will join you in a proper ceremony

8 The duel

First focus

1 *Mark the phrases that inform you about the course of events. Put down this information in note form in modern English.* →S13

_____
_____
_____
_____

> **TIP**
>
> A "**round character**" changes his behaviour or attitude throughout the play, while in contrast a "**flat character**" represents an unchanging type of "stock figure".

2 *Look at lines 116 ff. Underline Romeo's ideas that show his change of mind regarding violence. Refer back to Extract 4A, Task 2. Take down notes to prove that Romeo is a "round character".* →S7

_____
_____
_____
_____

3 *This scene takes place one hour after the wedding ceremony (lines 103 f). Evaluate whether or not Romeo is "fortune's fool".* →S14

_____
_____
_____
_____

Second focus

> **TIP**
>
> Use the copy of **Extract 8** to write your directions next to the lines.

4 *While today we depend strongly on visual input, in Elizabethan days people went to hear rather than to see a play relying more on words and sounds than on visual elements. Use the text as a basis for an e-book production. Write directions for the three very different characters on how to use their voices as well as when and how to incorporate exclamations, sounds, dramatic pauses, etc.* →S12

5 Creative writing: Benvolio orders Romeo to flee. Design an official warrant for Romeo on the run. Include information about his character, his role in the family feud, possible whereabouts, rewards promised by the Prince and the Capulets.

■ **In the meantime:** Shortly after the secret wedding, the feud between the two families flares up again, finding another climax in the death of Romeo's friend Mercutio who is stabbed in a duel by Tybalt. Romeo tries to separate the two opponents but does not succeed and the only thing he can do is to lament his friend's death. Then he meets Tybalt (cf. plot outline, Act III, ll. 1–9).

Romeo	This gentleman, the Prince's near ally[1],	100
	My very friend, hath got this mortal hurt	
	In my behalf; my reputation stained	
	With Tybalt's slander – Tybalt, that an hour	
	Hath been my cousin. O sweet Juliet,	
	Thy beauty hath made me effeminate[2],	105
	And in my temper[3] softened valour's steel!	
	(Enter Benvolio.)	
Benvolio	O Romeo, Romeo, brave Mercutio is dead.	
	That gallant spirit hath aspired[4] the clouds,	
	Which too untimely here did scorn the earth.	
Romeo	This day's black fate on moe days doth depend,	110
	This but begins the woe others must end.	
	(Enter Tybalt.)	
Benvolio	Here comes the furious Tybalt back again.	
Romeo	Again, in triumph, and Mercutio slain?	
	Away to heaven, respective lenity[5],	
	And fire-eyed fury be my conduct now!	115
	Now, Tybalt, take the 'villain' back again	
	That late thou gavest me, for Mercutio's soul	
	Is but a little way above our heads[6],	
	Staying for thine[7] to keep him company:	
	Either thou or I, or both, must go with him.	120
Tybalt	Thou wretched boy, that didst consort him here,	
	Shalt with him hence.	
Romeo	This shall determine that.	
	(They fight; Tybalt falls.)	
Benvolio	Romeo, away, be gone!	
	The citizens are up, and Tybalt slain.	
	Stand not amazed, the Prince will doom thee death[8]	125
	If thou art taken: Hence be gone, away!	
Romeo	O, I am fortune's fool[9].	
Benvolio	Why dost thou stay?	III, 1, 100–127

[1] **ally** *(here)* relative
[2] **effeminate** of female quality; *(here)* soft
[3] **temper** character
[4] **to aspire** to desire strongly
[5] **respective lenity** respectful softness
[6] **above our heads** *(here)* towards heaven
[7] **thine** yours
[8] **doom thee death** sentence you with the death penalty
[9] **fortune's fool** the toy of fate

✤ VERONA NEWS ✤

Romeo banished!

5 | Romeo and Juliet

9 Romeo banished

First focus

1 *Describe Juliet's problem in your own words on a separate sheet of paper.* →S14

2 *Mark five words or expressions in the text that help Juliet express her deep grief.* →S1

3 a) *Examine the four problems Juliet has to solve and the difficulties that arise from the solutions.*

Line	Problem	Difficulty
l. 97	Can I speak badly about my husband?	This would be illoyal and inappropriate.

b) *Discuss Juliet's alternatives.*

Second focus

4 *Select at least five of the images to visualise Juliet's states of mind at various stages in her speech. Connect them to the respective lines. Rehearse appropriate facial expressions in order to present these lines to the course.* →S28

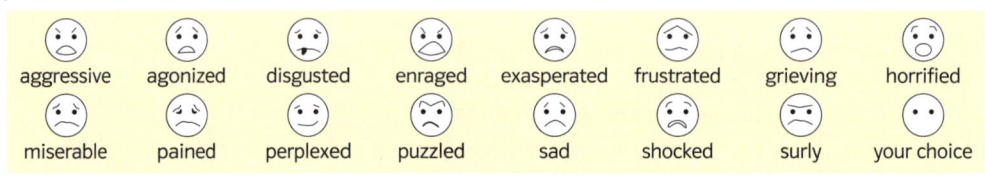

aggressive — agonized — disgusted — enraged — exasperated — frustrated — grieving — horrified
miserable — pained — perplexed — puzzled — sad — shocked — surly — your choice

■ **In the meantime:** Juliet has not received any information about the bloody events and is waiting for her newly married husband when the nurse informs her about the unfortunate, tragic turn of events (cf. plot outline, Act III, ll. 10–13).

Nurse	Will you speak well of him that killed your cousin?
Juliet	Shall I speak ill of him that is my husband?
	Ah, poor my lord, what tongue shall smooth thy name,
	When I, thy three-hours wife, have mangled¹ it?
	But wherefore, villain², didst thou kill my cousin? 100
	That villain cousin would have killed my husband.
	Back, foolish tears, back to your native spring,
	Your tributary drops³ belong to woe,
	Which you mistaking offer up to joy.
	My husband lives that Tybalt would have slain⁴ 105
	And Tybalt's dead that would have slain my husband:
	All this is comfort, wherefore weep I then?
	Some word there was, worser than Tybalt's death,
	That murdered me; I would forget it fain⁵,
	But O, it presses to my memory, 110
	Like damnèd guilty deeds to sinners' minds:
	'Tybalt is dead, and Romeo banishèd.'
	That 'banishèd', that one word 'banishèd',
	Hath slain ten thousand Tybalts. Tybalt's death
	Was woe enough if it had ended there; 115
	Or if sour woe delights in fellowship⁶,
	And needly⁷ will be ranked with other griefs,
	Why followed not, when she said 'Tybalt's dead',
	'Thy father' or 'thy mother', nay, or both,
	Which modern lamentation⁸ might have moved? III, 2, 96–120 120

¹ **mangled** destroyed
² **villain** Schurke
³ **tributary drops** tears giving respect
⁴ **slain** killed
⁵ **fain** with pleasure
⁶ **fellowship** partnership
⁷ **needly** necessarily
⁸ **modern lamentation** ordinary grief

Romeo and Juliet | 5

10 Consulting the Friar

First focus

1 [👥] *In four groups (A–D) work on these lines to answer the following questions. Which character traits does Friar Lawrence confront Romeo with? (**A**: ll. 108–121/ **B**: ll. 122–134)* →S23

A	Character traits	Line	Quote
	Romeo is a coward	l. 109	Art thou a man?
B	Romeo is lacking self-esteem	l. 122	Fie, fie, thou sham'st thy shape, thy love, …

*What does the Friar want Romeo to feel? (**C**: ll.135–145)* →S9

C	Expected emotion	Line	Quote
	build up more self-confidence	l. 135	What rouse thee, man! thy Juliet is alive,

*Describe Friar Lawrence's plan. (**D**: ll. 146–158)*

D	Steps in the plan	Line	Quote
	to go and see Juliet	l. 146	Go get the to thy love as was decreed,

2 *Analyse the values the Friar holds up in this scene.*

Values	Line	Quote
non-violence	l. 108	Hold thy desperate hand!
	l. 110 f.	
	l. 115	
	l. 120	
	l. 122	
	l. 127	
	l. 128	
	l. 129	

3 [👥] *Your teacher will give you a worksheet for this task. Work in groups and follow the instructions.*

5 | Romeo and Juliet

TIP

Use the copy of **Extract 10** to write your directions next to the lines.

Second focus

4 [👥] [👥👥] *You may want to do this exercise following Task 1. Divide the course into Friars and Romeos and team up in pairs. All Friars and all Romeos prepare the text by adding directions (cf. Extract 8, Second Focus) on the way the Friar's lines are to be presented and Romeo's reactions to them. Present your short scenes to the course and discuss the differences.*

■ **In the meantime:** Juliet has sent the nurse to bring Romeo to her. She finds him at Friar Lawrence's where she can just prevent Romeo from killing himself as he is devastated at being banished. The Friar unfolds a plan (cf. plot outline, Act II, ll. 14 – 17).

Friar Lawrence	Hold thy desperate hand!
	Art thou a man? thy form cries out thou art;
	Thy tears are womanish, thy wild acts denote 110
	The unreasonable fury of a beast.
	Unseemly woman in a seeming man,
	And ill-beseeming beast in seeming both,
	Thou hast amazed me. By my holy order,
	I thought thy disposition better tempered. 115
	Hast thou slain Tybalt? wilt thou slay thyself,
	And slay thy lady that in thy life lives,
	By doing damnèd hate upon thyself?
	Why rail'st thou[1] on thy birth? the heaven and earth?
	Since birth, and heaven, and earth, all three do meet 120
	In thee at once, which thou at once wouldst lose.
	Fie, fie, thou sham'st thy shape[2], thy love, thy wit,
	Which like a usurer[3] abound'st in all,
	And usest none in that true use indeed
	Which should bedeck[4] thy shape, thy love, thy wit: 125
	Thy noble shape is but a form of wax[5],
	Digressing[6] from the valour of a man;
	Thy dear love sworn but hollow perjury[7],
	Killing that love which thou hast vowed to cherish[8];
	Thy wit, that ornament to shape and love, 130
	Misshapen in the conduct of them both,
	Like powder in a skilless soldier's flask[9],
	Is set afire by thine own ignorance,
	And thou dismembered[10] with thine own defence.
	What, rouse thee, man! thy Juliet is alive, 135
	For whose dear sake thou wast but lately dead:
	There art thou happy. Tybalt would kill thee,
	But thou slewest Tybalt: there art thou happy.
	The law that threatened death becomes thy friend,
	And turns it to exile: there art thou happy. 140
	A pack of blessings light upon thy back,
	Happiness courts thee in her best array[11],
	But like a mishavèd[12] and sullen wench,
	Thou pouts[13] upon thy fortune and thy love:
	Take heed[14], take heed, for such die miserable. 145
	Go get thee to thy love as was decreed,
	Ascend her chamber, hence and comfort her;
	But look thou stay not till the Watch be set[15],
	For then thou canst not pass to Mantua,
	Where thou shalt live till we can find a time 150
	To blaze[16] your marriage, reconcile your friends,
	Beg pardon of the Prince, and call thee back
	With twenty hundred thousand times more joy
	Than thou went'st forth in lamentation[17].
	III, 3, 108 – 154

[1] **rail'st thou** do you complain
[2] **thou sham'st thy shape** you are a shame to your looks
[3] **usurer** person lending out money taking very high rates
[4] **to bedeck** to decorate
[5] **form of wax** soft copy
[6] **to digress** to move away from
[7] **perjury** telling a lie
[8] **vowed to cherish** promised to love
[9] **flask** *(here)* container for gunpowder
[10] **dismembered** cut into parts
[11] **array** arranged orderly
[12] **mishaved** misbehaved
[13] **pouts** *schmollen*
[14] **take heed** be careful
[15] **watch be set** wardens start their duty
[16] **to blaze** to publicise
[17] **lamentation** great sadness

■ **In the meantime:** The Nurse is sent back to Juliet and gives Romeo a ring from her.

Romeo and Juliet | 5

11 The lovers' farewell

First focus

1 a) *Note down in your own words what Romeo and Juliet talk about in lines 1–35. Mark the keywords in the text and copy them into the grid.* →S11

Line	What Romeo and Juliet talk about	Keywords
l. 2	perception of the time of day	nightingale, not the lark
l. 6		
l. 13		
l. 14		
l. 25		
l. 34		

b) Writing: *Now write a summary of this passage on a separate piece of paper.*

2 *Juliet is anxious about what this day might bring (lines 41–59). How do her words foreshadow death?* →S9, →S10

_____
_____
_____

3 *Which three images do you feel most appropriate to convey the idea of "upcoming death"?*

1. _____ 2. _____ 3. _____

Second focus

4 *For a modern theatre production the director has asked the course to suggest stage props for this scene. Select at least three props and justify your choice. Put down your ideas in note form.*

_____
_____

5 [👥] *This scene presents the last words Romeo and Juliet ever speak to each other alive. For the same theatre production note down your ideas of how to design a background curtain just for this scene. If you decide to work in a group, some may want to write down their ideas, others may want to draw a rough sketch of all the ideas you collect. Present your results in a gallery walk and praise the work with positive feedback only.* →S23
Alternative: Draw a cartoon of up to six pictures highlighting the tragic forebodings. →S22

6 Creative writing: *Having left Juliet, Romeo reflects on their last words ("…, and all these woes shall serve for sweet discourses in our times to come.", l. 52 f.). He decides to write a diary entry to remind himself of his emotional state at this moment for "times to come".* →S12

■ **In the meantime:** Because of Tybalt's death Lord Capulet has not talked to Juliet about his plan to marry her off to Paris. In the evening the Nurse has organised a step ladder to let Romeo enter Juliet's room undetected. It is the morning of their first night together (cf. plot outline, Act III, ll. 14–21).

> Juliet Wilt thou be gone? It is not yet near day:
> It was the nightingale[1], and not the lark[2],
> That pierced the fearful hollow of thine ear;
> Nightly she sings on yond pomegranate[3] tree.
> Believe me, love, it was the nightingale.   5

TIP

In Shakespeare's time there was no sophisticated stage scenery. The stage of the Globe remained mostly empty and unchanged. Parts of the bulding (e.g. columns) were used wherever needed. Only a very limited number of stage props was added. (cf. **Green Line Oberstufe Niedersachsen**, p. 224).

[1] **nightingale** *Nachtigall*
[2] **lark** *Lerche*
[3] **pomegranate** *Granatapfel*

5 Romeo and Juliet

Romeo	It was the lark, the herald of the morn,	
	No nightingale. Look, love, what envious[4] streaks	
	Do lace the severing clouds in yonder east:	
	Night's candles are burnt out, and jocund[5] day	
	Stands tiptoe on the misty mountain tops.	10
	I must be gone and live, or stay and die.	
Juliet	Yond light is not daylight, I know it, I:	
	It is some meteor that the sun exhaled[6]	
	To be to thee this night a torch-bearer,	
	And light thee on thy way to Mantua.	15
	Therefore stay yet, thou need'st not to be gone.	
Romeo	Let me be tane[7], let me be put to death,	
	I am content, so thou wilt have it so.	
	I'll say yon grey is not the morning's eye,	
	'Tis but the pale reflex of Cynthia's brow[8];	20
	Nor that is not the lark whose notes do beat	
	The vaulty[9] heaven so high above our heads.	
	I have more care to stay than will to go:	
	Come, death, and welcome! Juliet wills it so.	
	How is't, my soul? Let's talk, it is not day.	25
Juliet	It is, it is, hie hence, be gone, away!	
	It is the lark that sings so out of tune,	
	Straining harsh discords and unpleasing sharps.	
	Some say the lark makes sweet division[10]:	
	This doth not so, for she divideth us.	30
	Some say the lark and loathèd toad[11] changed eyes;	
	O now I would they had changed voices too,	
	Since arm from arm that voice doth us affray[12],	
	Hunting thee hence with hunt's-up[13] to the day.	
	O now be gone, more light and light it grows.	35
Romeo	More light and light, more dark and dark our woes!	
	(Enter nurse [hastily].)	
Nurse	Madam!	
Juliet	Nurse?	
Nurse	Your lady mother is coming to your chamber.	
	The day is broke, be wary, look about. *(Exit)*	40
Juliet	Then, window, let day in, and let life out.	
Romeo	Farewell, farewell! one kiss, and I'll descend.	
	(He goeth down.)	
Juliet	Art thou gone so, love, lord, ay husband, friend?	
	I must hear from thee every day in the hour,	
	For in a minute there are many days.	45
	O, by this count I shall be much in years[14]	
	Ere I again behold my Romeo!	
Romeo	*(From below)* Farewell!	
	I will omit no opportunity	
	That may convey my greetings, love, to thee.	50
Juliet	O think'st thou we shall ever meet again?	
Romeo	I doubt it not, and all these woes shall serve	
	For sweet discourses in our times to come.	
Juliet	O God, I have an ill-divining soul[15]!	
	Methinks[16] I see thee now, thou art so low,	55
	As one dead in the bottom of a tomb.	
	Either my eyesight fails, or thou look'st pale.	
Romeo	And trust me, love, in my eye so do you:	
	Dry sorrow[17] drinks our blood. Adieu, adieu! *(Exit)*	

III, 5, 1–59

[4] **envious** wanting sth that sb else has got
[5] **jocund** cheerful
[6] **some meteor that the sun exhaled** belief that meteors were fumes the sun lit up
[7] **tane** taken
[8] **reflex of Cynthia's brow** Cynthia = moon goddess
[9] **vaulty** ceiling in the form of an arch
[10] **division** *(here)* music
[11] **loathed toad** unpleasant frog
[12] **to affray** *(here)* to frighten
[13] **hunt's up** hunter's morning call
[14] **much in years** very old
[15] **ill-divining soul** bad expectations
[16] **methinks** I feel
[17] **dry sorrow** belief that each sigh cost blood

Romeo and Juliet   **5**

12 Violence in the family?

First Focus

1. a) *Note the development of Lord Capulet's anger in the grid and give quotes to support your notes.* →S9

Capulet's argumentation	Line	Quote
1. He first doesn't seem to understand that he has been challenged by Juliet.	l. 141 f.	…, take me with you, wife. How, will she none? doth she not give us thanks?
2.		
3.		
4.		
5.		
6.		

b) *Writing: Now describe the development of his anger on a separate piece of paper.*

2. *Vocabulary: Word bank "anger": Find five suitable words or expressions that illustrate the development of his emotions towards Juliet. Also refer back to the emoticons on page 96.* →S1

1. _surly_   2. _____   3. _____
4. _____   5. _____   6. _____

3. *Analyse Juliet's development as daughter (l. 158 f.), young woman and wife (ll. 196–203). On a separate piece of paper order your results as keywords in a grid.* →S7

4. *Writing: In an argumentative essay compare and contrast Capulet's idea of being a good father with a present-day idea of an ideal father. Use a separate sheet of paper.* →S14

Second focus

5. [👥] *Form groups of six. Using your results from Tasks 1 and 2, discuss how Lord Capulet confronts Juliet; think of what his body language will be and how he will speak (intensity and tone). Every member of the group takes one quote to present it to the group. The group suggests corrections if necessary and decides on one of the six words from the word bank "anger" to be matched to the quote. Each group member writes his word down on a separate sheet of paper.*
Now leave the classroom and select a stairway in your building. The members of each group place themselves on the stairs according to their impression of the intensity of anger Capulet expresses and showing their word and speaking their phrases accordingly.
The members of each group present ideas and finally agree upon the best solution.

■ **In the meantime:** In the morning Lady Capulet tells Juliet that she has been promised to Count Paris and will have to marry him that Thursday. Juliet rejects the parental order (cf. plot outline, Act III, ll. 21–26).

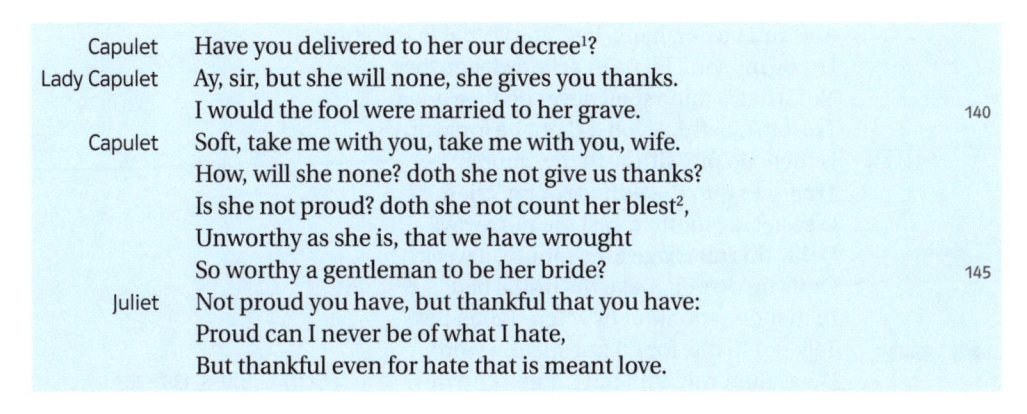

Capulet	Have you delivered to her our decree[1]?	
Lady Capulet	Ay, sir, but she will none, she gives you thanks.	
	I would the fool were married to her grave.	140
Capulet	Soft, take me with you, take me with you, wife.	
	How, will she none? doth she not give us thanks?	
	Is she not proud? doth she not count her blest[2],	
	Unworthy as she is, that we have wrought	
	So worthy a gentleman to be her bride?	145
Juliet	Not proud you have, but thankful that you have:	
	Proud can I never be of what I hate,	
	But thankful even for hate that is meant love.	

[1] **decree** order
[2] **blest** blessed

5 | Romeo and Juliet

Capulet	How how, how how, chopt-logic[3]? What is this?	
	'Proud', and 'I thank you', and 'I thank you not',	150
	And yet 'not proud', mistress minion[4] you?	
	Thank me no thankings, nor proud me no prouds,	
	But fettle your fine joints 'gainst[5] Thursday next,	
	To go with Paris to Saint Peter's Church,	
	Or I will drag thee on a hurdle[6] thither.	155
	Out, you green-sickness carrion[7]! out, you baggage!	
	You tallow[8]-face!	
Lady Capulet	Fie, fie, what, are you mad?	
Juliet	Good father, I beseech you on my knees,	
	Hear me with patience but to speak a word.	
	(She kneels down.)	
Capulet	Hang thee, young baggage, disobedient wretch!	160
	I tell thee what: get thee to church a'Thursday,	
	Or never after look me in the face.	
	Speak not, reply not, do not answer me!	
	My fingers itch. Wife, we scarce thought us blest	
	That God had lent us but this only child,	165
	But now I see this one is one too much,	
	And that we have a curse in having her.	
	Out on her, hilding[9]!	
Nurse	God in heaven bless her!	
	You are to blame, my lord, to rate[10] her so.	
Capulet	And why, my Lady Wisdom? Hold your tongue,	170
	Good Prudence, smatter[11] with your gossips, go.	
Nurse	I speak no treason.	
Capulet	O God-i-goden[12]!	
Nurse	May not one speak?	
Capulet	Peace, you mumbling fool!	
	Utter[13] your gravity[14] o'er a gossip's bowl[15],	
	For here we need it not.	
Lady Capulet	You are too hot.	175
Capulet	God's bread[16], it makes me mad! Day, night, work, play,	
	Alone, in company, still my care hath been	
	To have her matched; and having now provided	
	A gentleman of noble parentage,	
	Of fair demesnes[17], youthful and nobly ligned[18],	180
	Stuffed, as they say, with honourable parts,	
	Proportioned as one's thought would wish a man,	
	And then to have a wretched puling[19] fool,	
	A whining mammet[20], in her fortune's tender,	
	To answer 'I'll not wed, I cannot love;	185
	I am too young, I pray you pardon me.'	
	But and you will not wed, I'll pardon you:	
	Graze[21] where you will, you shall not house with me.	
	Look to't, think on't, I do not use to jest.	
	Thursday is near, lay hand on heart, advise:	190
	And you be mine, I'll give you to my friend;	
	And you be not, hang, beg, starve, die in the streets,	
	For by my soul, I'll ne'er acknowledge thee,	
	Nor what is mine shall never do thee good.	
	Trust to't, bethink you, I'll not be forsworn[22]. *(Exit)*	195
Juliet	Is there no pity sitting in the clouds	
	That sees into the bottom of my grief?	
	O sweet my mother, cast me not away!	
	Delay this marriage for a month, a week,	
	Or if you do not, make the bridal bed	200
	In that dim monument where Tybalt lies.	
Lady Capulet	Talk not to me, for I'll not speak a word.	
	Do as thou wilt, for I have done with thee. *(Exit)* III, 5, 138–203

[3] **chopt-logic** hacked logic; word games
[4] **minion** misbehaving *(spoilt)* child
[5] **fettle your fine joints 'gainst** be prepared for
[6] **hurdle** frame for dragging prisoners to their execution
[7] **green-sickness carrion** pale decaying meat
[8] **tallow** pale animal fat
[9] **hilding** useless person
[10] **to rate** to scold, to tell off
[11] **smatter** speak superficially
[12] **O God-i-godden** *(mockingly)* get going
[13] **to utter** to say
[14] **gravity** serious speech
[15] **gossip's bowl** *(here)* drinks at a ladies' party
[16] **God's bread** Hostie *(Fluch)*
[17] **demesnes** large area of land
[18] **ligned** ancestors, parentage
[19] **puling** wailing
[20] **mammet** puppet
[21] **to graze** to take food
[22] **to be forsworn** to break the oath

13 Visions of horror

First focus

1 *Write down in your own words what Juliet is prepared to do rather than marry Paris.*

_____
_____

2 *Explain what Friar Lawrence suggests Juliet should do (ll. 89–94) and to what effect (ll. 95–112).*

_____
_____

3 *Juliet is still only 13. On the basis of this scene assess the degree of adulthood she has reached.* →S14

Second focus

4 *To make the audience understand more clearly how desperate Juliet is, Shakespeare uses scary images they would be familiar with. To start with, find three lines with these images and write them on a separate sheet of paper. With the help of visual material of your choice, make a collage to illustrate the images using pictures expressing contemporary phobias and fears.* →S28

5 *Using your collages, argue the case why Shakespeare's language and images (though sometimes quite brutal) are so appealing to many people today.* →S26

■ **In the meantime:** Juliet does not know what to do and takes refuge at Friar Lawrence's who comes up with (yet another!) plan (cf. plot outline, Act IV, ll. 2–6).

Friar Lawrence	Hold, daughter, I do spy a kind of hope,
	Which craves¹ as desperate an execution
	As that is desperate which we would prevent.
	If, rather than to marry County Paris,
	Thou hast the strength of will to slay thyself,
	Then is it likely thou wilt undertake
	A thing like death to chide away this shame,
	That cop'st with² Death himself to scape³ from it;
	And if thou dar'st, I'll give thee remedy.
Juliet	O bid me leap, rather than marry Paris,
	From off the battlements⁴ of any tower,
	Or walk in thievish ways, or bid me lurk
	Where serpents are; chain me with roaring bears,
	Or hide me nightly in a charnel-house⁵,
	O'ercovered quite with dead men's rattling bones,
	With reeky shanks⁶ and yellow chapless⁷ skulls;
	Or bid me go into a new-made grave,
	And hide me with a dead man in his shroud –
	Things that to hear them told have made me tremble –
	And I will do it without fear or doubt,
	To live an unstained wife to my sweet love.
Friar Lawrence	Hold then, go home, be merry, give consent
	To marry Paris. Wednesday is tomorrow;
	Tomorrow night look that thou lie alone,
	Let not the Nurse lie with thee in thy chamber.
	Take thou this vial⁸, being then in bed,
	And this distilling liquor drink thou off,
	When presently through all thy veins shall run
	A cold and drowsy humour⁹; for no pulse
	Shall keep his native progress, but surcease¹⁰;
	No warmth, no breath shall testify thou livest; […]

¹ **to crave** to desire strongly
² **cop'st with** take it up
³ **to scape** to escape
⁴ **battlements** spaces on the top of a tower to shoot through
⁵ **charnel-house** place where human bones were stacked that had to make room for fresh graves
⁶ **reeky shanks** stinking leg bones *(between knee and ankle)*
⁷ **chapless** lacking a jawbone
⁸ **vial** a small glass container
⁹ **humour** liquid; *(here)* sensation
¹⁰ **no pulse … surcease** the pulse will stop its beating

5 Romeo and Juliet

Friar Lawrence	Now when the bridegroom in the morning comes To rouse thee from thy bed, there art thou dead. Then as the manner of our country is, In thy best robes, uncovered on the bier, Thou shall be borne to that same ancient vault Where all the kindred of the Capulets lie.

110

IV, 1, 68 – 98/107 – 112

14 Drama in Mantua

First focus

1 Describe in your own words how Romeo responds to the bad news Balthasar brings.

lines 13 – 16: Romeo is over-anxious and peppers Balthasar with questions.
___
___

2 Explain how Shakespeare manages to make Balthasar's remark "your looks are pale and wild" come to life by looking at the language in this passage. Mark and note down keywords.
___
___

3 *Writing:* Here is a definition of a tragic hero: "He goes blindly on an on and with every step he's spinning one more piece of thread which will eventually make up the network of his own tragedy." Discuss if this applies to Romeo. →S26

Second focus

4 *Creative writing:* News from Verona! Write Juliet's obituary for a tabloid newspaper. →S12

■ **In the meantime:** Following the Friar's advice Juliet pretends to give in and consents to the wedding with Paris, then takes the sleeping potion. She is found, believed to be dead. Her mourning family places her in the Capulets' tomb. Romeo is waiting for news from the Friar (cf. plot outline, Act IV, ll.7 – 14).

Romeo	News from Verona! How now, Balthasar? Dost thou not bring me letters from the Friar? How doth my lady? Is my father well? How doth my Juliet? That I ask again, For nothing can be ill if she be well.
Balthasar	Then she is well and nothing can be ill: Her body sleeps in Capels' monument¹, And her immortal part² with angels lives. I saw her laid low in her kindred's vault, And presently took post³ to tell it you. O pardon me for bringing these ill news, Since you did leave it for my office⁴, sir.
Romeo	Is it e'en so? then I defy you, stars! Thou knowest my lodging, get me ink and paper, And hire post-horses; I will hence tonight.
Balthasar	I do beseech you, sir, have patience: Your looks are pale and wild, and do import⁵ Some misadventure.
Romeo	Tush⁶, thou art deceived. Leave me, and do the thing I bid thee do. Hast thou no letters to me from the Friar?
Balthasar	No, my good lord.

15

20

25

30

¹ **Capel's monument** the Capulets' private burial vault
² **immortal part** soul
³ **presently took post** immediately got onto my way
⁴ **office** duty, obligation
⁵ **to import** to show signs of
⁶ **tush** quiet!
⁷ **means** Mittel
⁸ **apothecary** person who makes and sells medicine

Romeo	No matter, get thee gone,
	And hire those horses; I'll be with thee straight.
	(Exit [Balthasar])
	Well, Juliet, I will lie with thee tonight.
	Let's see for means⁷. O mischief, thou art swift 35
	To enter in the thoughts of desperate men!
	I do remember an apothecary⁸, V, 1, 12–37

15 The lovers' last words

First focus

1 *Express in your own words what death means to Romeo and Juliet in their situations.* → S14

Romeo: _____

_____

_____

_____

Juliet: _____

_____

_____

_____

> Put this in any liquid thing you will
> And drink it off, and if you had the strength
> Of twenty men, it would dispatch you straight

> Come, cordial and not poison, go with me
> To Juliet's grave, for there must I use thee.

2 *Romeo uses numerous metaphors in his speech. Choose the one you think best shows his state of mind.* → S10

_____

_____

TIP

For metaphor consult the *Glossary of literary terms* in **Green Line Oberstufe Niedersachsen**, p. 297.

3 *Writing:* On a separate sheet of paper, write a comment on the question whether their suicide is an act of free will. → S14

Second focus

4 *Consult with your art teacher (or do internet research) on pieces of art which you feel go well with this scene. Choose one and explain why you have chosen it.* → S32

■ **In the meantime:** Not having received the Friar's letter with the important information about the plan, Romeo believes Juliet to be dead and decides to return to be with her. At the tomb a grieving Paris tries to arrest Romeo. In their ensuing fight Romeo kills Paris and at his request puts his body next to Juliet before he himself decides to be reunited with his love in death (cf. plot outline, Act V, ll. 1–15).

Romeo	How oft when men are at the point of death
	Have they been merry, which their keepers¹ call
	A light'ning² before death! O how may I 90
	Call this a light'ning? O my love, my wife,
	Death, that hath sucked the honey of thy breath,
	Hath had no power yet upon thy beauty:
	Thou art not conquered, beauty's ensign³ yet
	Is crimson⁴ in thy lips and in thy cheeks, 95
	And Death's pale flag is not advanced there.
	Tybalt, liest thou there in thy bloody sheet?
	O, what more favour can I do to thee
	Than with that hand that cut thy youth in twain
	To sunder his that was thine enemy? 100

¹ **keepers** prison warden
² **light'ning** improving spirits
³ **ensign** flag on a ship
⁴ **crimson** dark red *(purpur)*

Romeo and Juliet

⁵ **paramour** *(lit)* lover
⁶ **yoke** Joch
⁷ **inauspicious** showing signs that the future will not be good
⁸ **engrossing** taking everything
⁹ **conduct** *(here)* poison
¹⁰ **unsavoury** unpleasant; morally not acceptable

Romeo	Forgive me, cousin. Ah, dear Juliet,	
	Why art thou yet so fair? Shall I believe	
	That unsubstantial Death is amorous,	
	And that the lean abhorrèd monster keeps	
	Thee here in dark to be his paramour⁵?	105
	For fear of that, I still will stay with thee,	
	And never from this palace of dim night	
	Depart again. Here, here will I remain	
	With worms that are thy chambermaids; O here	
	Will I set up my everlasting rest,	110
	And shake the yoke⁶ of inauspicious⁷ stars	
	From this world-wearied flesh. Eyes, look your last!	
	Arms, take your last embrace! and, lips, O you	
	The doors of breath, seal with a righteous kiss	
	A dateless bargain to engrossing⁸ Death!	115
	Come, bitter conduct⁹, come, unsavoury¹⁰ guide!	
	Thou desperate pilot, now at once run on	
	The dashing rocks thy seasick weary bark!	
	Here's to my love! *(Drinks.)* O true apothecary!	
	Thy drugs are quick. Thus with a kiss I die. *(Dies.)* V, 3, 88 – 120	120

■ **In the meantime:** The Friar has found Paris and Romeo dead and when Juliet awakes he has to break the news to her

Friar Lawrence	*(Enters the tomb.)*	
	Romeo! O, pale! Who else? What, Paris too?	
	And steeped in blood? Ah, what an unkind hour	
	Is guilty of this lamentable chance!	145
	(Juliet rises.)	
	The lady stirs.	
Juliet	O comfortable Friar, where is my lord?	
	I do remember well where I should be;	
	And there I am. Where is my Romeo?	150
	(Noise within.)	
Friar Lawrence	I hear some noise, lady. Come from that nest	
	Of death, contagion, and unnatural sleep.	
	A greater power than we can contradict	
	Hath thwarted our intents. Come, come away.	
	Thy husband in thy bosom there lies dead;	155
	And Paris too. Come, I'll dispose of thee	
	Among a sisterhood of holy nuns.	
	Stay not to question, for the Watch is coming.	
	Come go, good Juliet, I dare no longer stay. *(Exit)*	
Juliet	Go get thee hence, for I will not away.	160
	What's here? a cup closed in my true love's hand?	
	Poison I see hath been his timeless end.	
	O churl, drunk all, and left no friendly drop	
	To help me after? I will kiss thy lips,	
	Haply some poison yet doth hang on them,	165
	To make me die with a restorative.	
	Thy lips are warm.	
Captain of the watch	*(Within)* Lead, boy, which way?	
Juliet	Yea, noise? Then I'll be brief. O happy dagger,	
	(Taking Romeo's dagger.)	
	This is thy sheath; *(Stabs herself.)*	
	there rust, and let me die.	170
	(Falls on Romeo's body and dies.) V, 3, 144 – 170	

Romeo and Juliet | 5

16 The tragic remains

First focus

1 *Looking at lines 292f., state briefly what the Prince means by "heaven finds means to kill your joys with love". →S26*

_____
_____
_____

2 a) *Mark and quote expressions that help you to analyse the atmosphere of this final scene. →S10*

Line	Quote	Atmosphere
l. 287	… the tidings of her death	sorrow, empathy
l. 292		

b) *Use your results to write a brief description of the atmosphere on a separate piece of paper.*

3 *The principle of tragedy is that the hero dies at the end of the play. Collect reasons and discuss why as the heroes, Romeo and Juliet inevitably have to die.*

_____
_____
_____
_____

Second focus

4 [👥] *"For never was a story of more woe than this of Juliet and her Romeo". In groups of 5–6 select about 10 different scenes that tell the story and rehearse them as freeze frames. All the members of the group have to take any part in every individual frame. Present your frames and let the other groups guess what your human picture stands for. You might like to take photographs and add words to them thus creating a photo story of your own. →S23*

■ **In the meantime:** The Watch has arrested the Friar at the tomb. Lord Capulet and Lord Montague enter the tomb to see their dead children. The Prince promises to shed light onto the tragedy and to give verdicts. The Friar informs them all about the chain of events and his plan. The Prince believes his words when he reads Romeo's letter (cf. plot outline, Act V, ll. 18–24).

Prince	This letter doth make good the Friar's words,	
	Their course of love, the tidings of her death;	
	And here he writes that he did buy a poison	
	Of a poor pothecary, and therewithal[1]	
	Came to this vault to die, and lie with Juliet.	290
	Where be these enemies? Capulet, Montague?	
	See what a scourge[2] is laid upon your hate,	
	That heaven finds means to kill your joys[3] with love!	
	And I for winking at your discords[4] too	
	Have lost a brace of kinsmen[5]. All are punished.	295
Capulet	O brother Montague, give me thy hand.	
	This is my daughter's jointure[6], for no more	
	Can I demand.	

[1] **therewithal** by this *(i.e. the poison)*
[2] **scourge** a person that causes suffering *(Geißel)*
[3] **joys** *(here)* feuding
[4] **winking at your discords** not paying attention to your fighting
[5] **kinsmen** *(here)* Mercutio and Paris
[6] **jointure** Mitgift

Romeo and Juliet

Montague	But I can give thee more,
	For I will raise her statue in pure gold,
	That whiles Verona by that name is known,
	There shall no figure at such rate be set[7]
	As that of true and faithful Juliet.
Capulet	As rich shall Romeo's by his lady's lie,
	Poor sacrifices of our enmity[8]!
Prince	A glooming peace this morning with it brings,
	The sun for sorrow will not show his head.
	Go hence to have more talk of these sad things;
	Some shall be pardoned, and some punishèd:
	For never was a story of more woe
	Than this of Juliet and her Romeo.
	(*Exeunt omnes*[9])

V, 3, 286–310

[7] **at such rate be set** seen at such value
[8] **enmity** hatred towrds sb
[9] **exeunt omnes** all leave

C More on the play

1 Mediation: *In your course you have been looking into the question of how Shakespeare's plays can be presented on the stage. During your research you have come across an article about a Shakespeare production by the* Parkaue Club 4 *of the* Junger Berliner Staatstheater.
You write an email (about 250 words) to the Education Department of the Globe Theatre in London, outlining the special features of the production and asking them whether they feel this kind of production does justice to Shakespeare's work. Write the email on a separate piece of paper.

Crashkurs Shakespeare

Riskant gepokert vom Parkaue Club 4 des Jungen Berliner Staatstheaters: Romeo und Julia wollen sie machen, da müssen die Einsätze hoch sein und der Text ernst genommen werden. Lieber hätten sie sich an eine Eigenproduktion gewagt, wird sich gleich zu Beginn entschuldigt, zum Thema „Zukunft" zum Beispiel, Abi, Umweltschutz oder so. Aber einfach keine Zeit während all der Prüfungen, da musste eben die literarische Vorlage ran. Diese ewige Geschichte über zwei verfeindete Häuser mit zwei verliebten Menschen, die erst zusammen sind, dann doch wieder nicht, dann wieder doch und am Ende sind alle tot. Der Chor tritt auf, der alte Groll Veronas wird aufs Neue heraufbeschworen. Doch lange geht das nicht gut.

„Ich kann hier nicht so eine Scheiße spielen", tönt einer, der Streit verlässt Verona und betritt die Bühne. Arbeitslicht an, jetzt wird erst mal diskutiert, was hier gemacht wird und warum. Das ist ironischerweise auch genau das Spiel-im-Spiel, das wir schon von Shakespeare kennen, das Vexierspiel zwischen Sein und Schein, die Probe im Stück; bei Hamlet, Othello oder dem Sommernachtstraum. Es ist eben dieses Spiel im Spiel und keine performative Form, die gewählt wird. Es wird nicht aus der Rolle gefallen, weil nie wirklich eine da war und privat wird es auch nicht. Die vermeintlichen Privatheiten werden gesprochen wie Text und der Text, wenn er denn mal kommt, wie Privatheiten. Was ist wahr und was nicht? Eine Diskussion entspinnt sich um die Frage: Was soll der alte Stoff noch von uns und heute erzählen, rauscht er nicht gnadenlos an uns vorbei?

[23] **Vexierspiel** *wechselseitiges Durchdringen*

Ins Mikro der verzweifelte Hilfeschrei an die allerhöchsten Ämter: Gott und die Regie sollen helfen. Das tun sie tatsächlich, mit allen Mitteln, die ihnen zur Verfügung stehen: Romantisches Licht, die Dudelmusik, Amor, der eigentlich die Lina mit-Flügelchen ist, schießt seine Pfeile. Damit haben die Parkauer Jungs und Mädchen nicht gerechnet, sie sterben unter bestialischen Schmerzen den Liebestod. Das Ineinander-Greifen, die Überlagerung von Stoff und Probe erreicht den höchsten Punkt: die unerklärliche Liebe, die schicksalhafte, die von Shakespeare, die man sich vielleicht gern erspart hätte (und damit alle die Probleme), wird zur Realität der Spielerinnen und Spieler. Sie befinden sich zwischen Probe und Spiel, alles zur Hälfte angedeutet, zur Hälfte der volle Ernst. Überfallartig dringt ab und an der alte Text in ihre Münder, streut seine Sentenzen: Sie können ihm nicht mehr entkommen.
In der Dunkelheit, nur mit Taschenlampen-Beleuchtung, werden die ersten, zarten Banden geknüpft. Wir sind gleichzeitig mit Taschenlampen unter ihren Bettdecken, als auch im theatralen Maskenspiel. Gegenseitig wird sich die Liebe gestanden, alle kommen irgendwie unter, bis auf einen, der sucht wohl heute noch. Da wird ein flacher Witz nach dem anderen abgefeuert, alles ist heiter und ehrlich ironisch. Die Schwellenangst vor Romeo und Julia überträgt sich auf die Anbahnungsversuche und dann wiederum auf das Spiel im Spiel. Das ist ungezwungen, souverän und es macht Spaß, zuzuschauen. Ein Liedchen wird gesungen, wenn auch nicht aus vollem Hals, das Playback muss es tun. Und wo ist eigentlich diese Lina?
Auch hier geht es natürlich nicht ewig weiter, der Tag nach der ersten Nacht kündigt sich an. Grell und irgendwie anders als vorher, sieht man sich selbst und die anderen. Der Zauber ist verflogen. Es wird sich getrennt und verlassen, Amor hat keine Pfeiler mehr im Köcher. Auch das Publikum muss gleich den Saal verlassen: Hier ist alles vorbei. Nur den Shakespeare hat man jetzt irgendwie vergessen. Kein Problem, den braucht nun wirklich niemand. Jedenfalls nicht mehr, als einfach den extrem charmanten Parkauer Jungs und Mädchen zuzuschauen, die in ihrer nur 33-minütigen Produktion in aller Kürze ganz viel von dem verhandeln, was Jugendtheater sein kann, wie Umgang mit Klassikern sein kann oder, um nicht zu hoch zu greifen: Wie man befreit und humorvoll, unaufgeregt und ehrlich eine Bühne betreten kann. Dass die Themen dann doch etwas abgegriffen, nur angeschnitten daherkamen, sich kein großes, innerliches Nachbeben einstellte: Geschenkt. Super!

blog.theatertreffen-der-jugend.de

2 *Listening: The text you are about to hear is on the CD in **Green Line Oberstufe Niedersachsen** (Topic 16 "Shakespeare on the silver screen"). In it James Hansen, a director, and Brent Keyes, an actor and director, are speculating on Shakespeare as a moviemaker.* → S21

After you have listened to the text once, note whether the sentences are true or false. You will hear the excerpt again, after which you will have a minute to check your answers.

James Hansen says …

1. Shakespeare was the Lord Chamberlain. _____
2. The Globe Theatre had a thousand seats. _____
3. The emotion, humour and spectacle of Shakespeare's plays were too much for his audiences. _____
4. You can compare Shakespeare with today's famous film directors. _____

Brent Keyes says …

5. You can't enter the life of a character in a film the way you can do it on stage. _____
6. Through the new techniques cinema turns old material into something new. _____
7. He thinks Shakespeare would have been open to the possibilities in today's media. _____
8. Cinema rewrites Shakespeare's plays in order to reinterpret them. _____

Chapter 6 — *The Merchant of Venice*

TIP

You can find basic information on Shakespeare himself, his works and his language in **Green Line Oberstufe Niedersachsen**, Topic 16.

TIP

Read the handout with the **plot outline** carefully and use it as a source of information when working with further excerpts from the play.

A Shakespeare for starters

Because Shakespeare was a wonderful storyteller his works are still appreciated today all over the world. Using powerful language he deals with topics which are still right up to date. His plays are performed traditionally or interpreted in modern adaptations by countless theatres around the globe and enjoyed by large audiences. The universal appeal of his works offers timeless insights into problems and their unexpected solutions.

We want to show you ways of exploring Shakespeare on your own with the guiding help of assignments in a twofold way. First Focus: the understanding of selected scenes and Second Focus: the "physical approach" where you are invited to get involved personally.

Our selection of scenes stresses the problems encountered in a "clash of cultures". What would you do if a harmless deal suddenly turns out to be life threatening? Antonio, a merchant of Venice, and Shylock, a Jewish moneylender, carry their feud to extremes when negotiating a potentially fatal deal.

1 *With the help of the plot outline provided by your teacher match the characters to the descriptions given below.*

Antonio • Shylock • Bassiano • Graziano • Portia • Nerissa • Jessica • Lorenzo • Prince of Morocco

1. Wealthy heiress, who disguises herself _____
2. Merchant with a loving heart _____
3. Sly moneylender looking out for revenge _____
4. Playboy with no financial means _____
5. Egocentric suitor to a rich lady _____
6. Disobedient daughter to tyrannical father _____

The Merchant of Venice

7. Supports a friend and finds a wife _____

8. Woman in waiting who believes in love _____

9. Is rewarded after stealing a fortune _____

2 [👥] *Get together with a partner, choose a line and speak it out loud together. To find its rhythm, it might help if you link hands and make a "see-saw" movement. Describe what you feel is special about your line or what the line may tell you.*

Shylock	You called me dog: and for these courtesies	
	I'll lend you thus much monies.	I, 3, 120 f.
Shylock	Let not the sound of shallow foppery enter my sober house.	II, 5, 34 f.
Salarino	There is more difference between thy flesh and hers	
	than between jet and ivory; more between your bloods	
	than there is between red wine and Rhenish.	III, 1, 31 ff.
Shylock	He hath disgraced me, and hindered me half a million,	
	laughed at my losses, mocked at my gains, scorned my nation,	
	thwarted my bargains, cooled my friends, heated mine enemies	
	– and what's his reason? I am a Jew. Hath not a Jew eyes?	
	Hath not a Jew hands, organs, dimensions, senses,	
	affections, passions?	III, 1, 43 ff.
Antonio	An evil soul producing holy witness	
	Is like a villain with a smiling cheek,	
	A goodly apple rotten at the heart	
	O what a goodly outside falsehood hath!	I, 3, 91 ff.
Gratiano	Not on thy sole, but on thy soul, harsh Jew,	
	Thou mak'st thy knife keen.	IV, 1, 123 f.
Portia	The quality of mercy is not strained,	
	It droppeth as the gently rain from heaven	IV, 1, 180 f.
Portia	Since you are dear bought, I will love you dear.	III, 2, 312
Portia	What mercy can you render him, Antonio?	
Gratiano	A halter gratis – nothing else, for God's sake.	IV, 1, 374 f.
Portia	If you had known the virtue of the ring,	
	Or half her worthiness that gave the ring,	
	Or your own honour to contain the ring,	
	You would not then have parted with the ring.	V, 1, 199
Bassiano	What demi-god hath come so near creation?	III, 2, 115 f.

TIP

Rhythm and metre of Shakespeare's writing
One of the fundamental insights into Shakespeare's language is its regular rhythm or beat which is very helpful for the understanding of his plays. The main metre of Shakespeare's writing was a regular rhythm of five units of an unstressed and stressed word, called an iamb. This unit is quite similar to a single heart beat (dee-dum). If you want to imitate Shakespeare's rhythm you try to write lines with five regular stresses, e.g.: dee-dum / dee-dum / dee-dum / dee-dum / dee-dum.

How to start enjoying Shakespeare's texts – basic exercises

1. Get together in a circle and read the text aloud "in a round" everyone reading one word only.

2. Read the text again. Now everyone reads to the next punctuation mark.

3. Now read line by line while those who do not read tap the metre with their hands.

4. Walk around the room speaking one line at a time and at the end of it make a sharp 90 degree turn.

5. Do it again but now turn at every punctuation mark and turn at full stops.

6. The next time only turn when everyone individually feels the end of a sense unit.

7. Finally, from where you are recite the whole passage in whatever way you think right. You may sing, whisper, shout or do whatever you believe to be appropriate.

6 | The Merchant of Venice

B Selected extracts and assignments

1 Development of plot structure I (Introduction)

First focus

TIP

Working with the texts
To help you understand them better, always read the texts both silently and aloud.
When you are doing the assignments in **First focus**, mark in the text important passages or keywords you will need for the solutions.

1 *Read the text below and give a precise account of Shylock's main points.*
Antonio is _____
_____
_____

2 a) *Vocabulary:* To start a word bank on the topic of "hate and disgust" find five expressions from the text. →S1
   1. _____ 2. _____ 3. _____
              4. _____ 5. _____

   b) *Explain which values Shylock discusses. Write down a ranking order and justify your decision.*

   • _____
   • _____
   • _____
   • _____

Second focus

TIP

In **Second Focus** we offer different approaches to working with a longer dramatic text.
To make the work with Shakespeare's texts easier, more effective and rewarding, you should start by reading them aloud. Shakespeare did not write his texts to be learned by heart, he wrote them to be performed on stage. You may want to try out your own versions (see **Basic exercises** on page 111).

3 [👥] *The speech below is an aside, Shylock talks to the audience only and is not heard by Antonio. To get an impression of the effect this technique has on you/the audience, one of you reads the text aloud and slowly while the partner – without looking at the text – echoes those words that he/she feels express Shylock's hatred towards Antonio. Change partners twice to repeat the exercise.*

4 *This passage from Act I Scene III presents the overall ethical problem of the play. After you have practised coming to terms with the passage by reading it aloud, try out a number of alternative ways of speaking. Then work out the particular choice of words which gives this passage its hostile tone. Mark these keywords in the text.*

5 *Discuss the impression you got of the reasons for Shylock's aggression.*

6 *Writing:* Write an aside that Antonio might speak to the audience about his opinion of Shylock. Try to achieve a similar style and rhythm. →S10, →S12

7 [👥] *Having written an aside for Antonio, perform it in front of the class with your partner. One of you reads Shylock's lines, the other one those of Antonio. Speak one line at a time.*

¹ **fawning** trying to get attention by flattery
² **publican** *(here)* taxman
³ **usance** fee taken for lent money
⁴ **ancient** very old
⁵ **grudge** unfriendly feelings
⁶ **to rail** to criticise sth vehemently
⁷ **to congregate** to get together in a group
⁸ **thrift** ability of keeping money together
⁹ **interest** money paid as a result of depositing or lending money
¹⁰ **Cursed be my tribe** May God curse my people

Bassanio	This is Signor Antonio.
Shylock	*(Aside)* How like a fawning¹ publican² he looks!
	I hate him for he is a Christian;
	But more, for that in low simplicity 35
	He lends out money gratis, and brings down
	The rate of usance³ here with us in Venice.
	If I can catch him once upon the hip,
	I will feed fat the ancient⁴ grudge⁵ I bear him.
	He hates our sacred nation, and he rails⁶ 40
	Even there where merchants most do congregate⁷
	On me, my bargains, and my well-won thrift⁸
	Which he calls interest⁹. Cursed be my tribe¹⁰
	If I forgive him! I, 3, 32–44

The Merchant of Venice | 6

2 The antagonists

First focus

1. a) *Read the text, then, on a separate piece of paper, make two lists of positive and negative qualities to describe the differences between Antonio and Shylock (ll. 89–129).* →S1, →S7
   b) *In your own words describe how Antonio sees Shylock. Make use of your word bank on "hate and disgust" by adding relevant expressions.*
   c) *First explain why Shylock can be considered as a "villain with a smiling cheek". Then find one example of a modern representative that in your eyes fits this description.*

2. *Make a list of the ways Antonio usually treats Shylock (ll. 98–122).*

   _____

   _____

3. a) *Analyse the views the two characters have on charging interest (ll. 124–135).*

   Antonio: _____

   Shylock: _____

   b) *Assess the suggestion that the bond is a "merry sport" in the light of your knowledge about a "villain with a smiling cheek" (ll. 136–146).*

   _____

   _____

   _____

   c) *Discuss if enemies can buy "friendship" in a situation of mutual interest (ll. 147–164).* →S26

Second focus

4. *A new TV production of "The Merchant of Venice" is asking schools for ideas for new ways of producing and interpreting this particular scene.*
   a) [👥] *With your partner go through the scene and perform these lines to illustrate the significance of particular textual elements.*
   b) *Write directions for the actors on the handout provided by your teacher.*
   c) [👥] *In groups of 3 to 4 discuss your results and and make suggestions as to which elements you would like to see in a final production.*
   d) *Produce your versions with the help of a camcorder and select the one the course agrees upon to be the best.* →S23

> **TIP**
>
> Use the copy of **Extract 2** your teacher will give you for your stage directions.

Antonio	Mark you this, Bassanio,
	The devil can cite Scripture for his purpose. 90
	An evil soul producing holy witness
	Is like a villain with a smiling cheek,
	A goodly apple rotten at the heart.
	O what a goodly outside falsehood hath!
Shylock	Three thousand ducats, 'tis a good round sum. 95
	Three months from twelve, then let me see, the rate –
Antonio	Well, Shylock, shall we be beholding¹ to you?
Shylock	Signor Antonio, many a time and oft
	In the Rialto² you have rated me
	About my monies and my usances. 100
	Still have I borne it with a patient shrug³
	For suff'rance is the badge⁴ of all our tribe.
	You call me misbeliever, cut-throat dog,
	And spit upon my Jewish gaberdine⁵,
	And all for use of that which is mine own. 105
	Well then, it now appears you need my help.

¹ **beholding** indebted
² **Rialto** centre of commerce in Venice
³ **shrug** raising and lowering one's shoulders
⁴ **badge** sign
⁵ **gaberdine** thick cloth for coats

The Merchant of Venice

Shylock	Go to, then, you come to me, and you say,	
	'Shylock, we would have monies' – you say so,	
	You that did void your rheum⁶ upon my beard,	
	And foot me as you spurn a stranger cur⁷	110
	Over your threshold⁸: monies is your suit.	
	What should I say to you? Should I not say	
	'Hath a dog money? Is it possible	
	A cur can lend three thousand ducats?' Or	
	Shall I bend low, and in a bondman's key,	115
	With bated breath⁹ and whispering humbleness,	
	Say this:	
	'Fair sir, you spat on me on Wednesday last,	
	You spurned me such a day, another time	
	You called me dog: and for these courtesies	120
	I'll lend you thus much monies.'	
Antonio	I am as like to call thee so again,	
	To spit on thee again, to spurn thee too.	
	If thou wilt lend this money, lend it not	
	As to thy friends, for when did friendship take	125
	A breed for barren¹⁰ metal of his friend?	
	But lend it rather to thine¹¹ enemy,	
	Who if he break¹², thou mayst with better face	
	Exact¹³ the penalty.	
Shylock	Why look you how you storm!	130
	I would be friends with you, and have your love,	
	Forget the shames that you have stained me with,	
	Supply your present wants, and take no do it	
	Of usance¹⁴ for my monies, and you'll not hear me.	
	This is kind I offer.	
Bassanio	This were kindness.	135
Shylock	This kindness will I show.	
	Go with me to a notary, seal me there	
	Your single bond¹⁵, and, in a merry sport,	
	If you repay me not on such a day,	
	In such a place, such sum or sums as are	140
	Expressed in the condition, let the forfeit¹⁶	
	Be nominated for an equal pound	
	Of your fair flesh, to be cut off and taken	
	In what part of your body pleaseth me.	
Antonio	Content, in faith! I'll seal to such a bond,	145
	And say there is much kindness in the Jew.	
Bassanio	You shall not seal to such a bond for me;	
	I'll rather dwell¹⁷ in my necessity.	
Antonio	Why, fear not, man, I will not forfeit it.	
	Within these two months, that's a month before	150
	This bond expires¹⁸, I do expect return	
	Of thrice¹⁹ three times the value of this bond.	
Shylock	O father Abram, what these Christians are,	
	Whose own hard dealings teaches them suspect	
	The thoughts of others! Pray you tell me this:	155
	If he should break his day what should I gain	
	By the exaction of the forfeiture?	
	A pound of man's flesh, taken from a man,	
	Is not so estimable²⁰, profitable²¹ neither,	
	As flesh of muttons²², beefs or goats. I say	160
	To buy his favour, I extend this friendship	
	If he will take it, so; if not, adieu,	
	And for my love, I pray you wrong me not.	
Antonio	Yes, Shylock, I will seal unto this bond.	I, 3, 89–164

⁶ **to void your rheum** to spit
⁷ **cur** frightening dog of mixed race
⁸ **threshhold** doorstep
⁹ **with bated breath** in an excited way
¹⁰ **barren** unfruitful
¹¹ **thine** *(arch)* your
¹² **to break** not to pay back in time
¹³ **to exact** to get sth by force
¹⁴ **no doit of usance** no extra money to be paid
¹⁵ **bond** legal contract
¹⁶ **forfeit** punishment
¹⁷ **to dwell** to live
¹⁸ **to expire** to run out of time
¹⁹ **thrice** three times
²⁰ **not estimable** difficult to measure
²¹ **profitable** to result in a profit
²² **mutton** meat from a grown sheep

The Merchant of Venice 6

3 Developing profiles

First focus

1 *Vocabulary:* With the help of a monolingual dictionary explore the meaning of the words "sober" and "sobriety". →S3

sober	sobriety

2 *Read the text and explain in your own words what Shylock means by "my sober house" in the context of this scene.*

_____
_____

3 *Continue the list of Shylock's qualities (cf. Extract 2, Task 1a).*

_____
_____

Second focus

4 [👥] *Here Shylock is giving Lancelot and Jessica his views on life. Act out this little scene in groups of three, making use of body language and facial expressions. Variations: Some groups are can use more extrovert forms of expression, while others have to be moderate.* →S7

Shylock	What, are there masques? Hear you me, Jessica,		
	Lock up my doors, and when you hear the drum		
	And the vile[1] squealing[2] of the wry-necked fife[3],		
	Clamber[4] not you up to the casements then	30	
	Nor thrust your head into the public street		
	To gaze on Christian fools with varnished faces;		
	But stop[5] my house's ears – I mean my casements –		
	Let not the sound of shallow foppery enter		
	My sober house. By Jacob's staff[6] I swear	35	
	I have no mind of feasting forth[7] tonight:		
	But I will go. Go you before me, sirrah[8];		
	Say I will come.		
Lancelot	I will go before, sir.		
	(Aside to Jessica) Mistress, look out at window for all this:		
	There will come a Christian by	40	
	Will be worth a Jewès eye *(Exit)*		
Shylock	What says that fool of Hagar's[9] offspring, ha?		
Jessica	His words were 'Farewell, mistress', nothing else.		
Shylock	The patch[10] is kind enough, but a huge feeder[11],		
	Snail-slow in profit, and he sleeps by day	45	
	More than the wildcat. Drones[12] hive not with me,		
	Therefore I part with him, and part with him		
	To one that I would have him help to waste		
	His borrowed purse[13]. Well, Jessica, go in;		
	Perhaps I will return immediately.	50	
	Do as I bid you, shut doors after you.		
	Fast bind, fast find:		
	A proverb never stale[14] in thrifty mind. *(Exit)*		
Jessica	Farewell, and if my fortune be not crossed,		
	I have a father, you a daughter, lost. *(Exit)*	II, 5, 27–55	55

[1] **vile** unpleasant
[2] **squealing** high pitched sound
[3] **wry necked fife** a badly played flute
[4] **to clamber** to climb up
[5] **to stop** to close
[6] **staff** stick to give support when walking
[7] **feasting forth** going out for dinner
[8] **sirrah** archaic term to address inferiors
[9] **Hagar's offspring** child of Hagar, Abraham's maid
[10] **patch** fool
[11] **huge feeder** person who eats a lot
[12] **drones** male bee
[13] **borrowed purse** not his own money *(he refers to Bassanio)*
[14] **stale** not fresh

115

6 | The Merchant of Venice

5 *Looking at Shylock's and Jessica's behaviour, where would you place them in the table below? Justify your answers.*

0 % Steps towards integration: 100 %

Denial – i.e. total rejection of the dominant culture.	**Defence** – recognition of cultural differences yet negative evaluation.	**Minimisation** – minimal acceptance of basic values, differences.	**Acceptance** – recognition of differences in behaviour and values.	**Adaptation** – development of skills of intercultural communication.	**Integration** – total acceptance of dominant culture.

TIP

Steps towards integration
Sociological studies have tried to define the degree to which members of minorities have shown their acceptance of the culture they live in. This chart denotes different stages of acceptance (adapted from Milton Bennett).

_____
_____

6 *In three different extracts Shylock has so far shown three different facets of his character. Outline the main features of these facets.*

I, 3, 32 – 44 _____

I, 3, 89 – 164 _____

II, 5, 27 – 55 _____

4 Development of plot structure II (Rising action)

First focus

"Who chooseth me, shall gain what many men desire."

"Who chooseth me, shall get as much as he deserves."

"Who chooseth me, must give and hazard all he hath."

1 *You work for an advertising agency. The company wants to promote products with the help of catchy slogans. Find examples of products which would benefit most from one of the three slogans on the caskets on the left (ll. 1 – 10).*

gold: _____

silver: _____

lead: _____

2 a) *Explain what it means:*

1. the desire for a beloved person: _____
_____

2. the feeling of deserving a beloved person: _____
_____

3. to risk everything you have for the beloved person: _____
_____

b) *Read the text and describe how the Prince sees himself and Portia.*

Prince of Morocco	Portia

116

The Merchant of Venice   6

c) *Compare his and her qualities in a ranking list to the qualities of a present day famous couple.*

_____
_____
_____
_____

Second focus

3 *Imagine Queen Elizabeth I is present in the theatre. You are the Prince of Morocco, the future King of Morocco. Address her with this speech (ll. 15 – 60) and be as royal as you can.* → S15

4 *You are going to take part in a dating show. You will have to convince the person who you want to date of your qualities. To do so write a mini saga (exactly 50 words) praising yourself with some of the ideas from Morocco's speech.* → S12

_____
_____
_____
_____
_____
_____
_____
_____
_____
_____

5 [👥] *Creative writing: According to the conditions of the lottery, if the Prince woos Portia in vain, he is not allowed to ask any lady to marry him. He consults his best friend beforehand about what to do. Write a dialogue between the two men and act out the scene.* → S12

6 *After opening the casket the Prince is desolate. One part of the class reads the words on the scroll (ll. 65 – 73) in his manner, while the others echo his words in the fashion of very uncomplimentary and mean groundlings mocking him at his departure.*

Portia	Go, draw aside the curtains and discover	
	The several caskets[1] to the noble prince.	
	Now make your choice.	
Morocco	This first of gold, who this inscription bears,	
	'Who chooseth me, shall gain what many men desire.'	5
	The second silver, which this promise carries,	
	'Who chooseth me, shall get as much as he deserves.'	
	This third dull lead, with warning all as blunt[2],	
	'Who chooseth me, must give and hazard[3] all he hath.'	
	How shall I know if I do choose the right?	10
Portia	The one of them contains my picture, prince.	
	If you choose that, then I am yours withal.	
Morocco	Some god direct my judgement! Let me see:	
	I will survey[4] th'inscriptions back again.	
	What says this leaden casket?	15
	"Who chooseth me, must give and hazard all he hath."	
	Must give – for what? For lead? Hazard for lead!	
	This casket threatens: men that hazard all	
	Do it in hope of fair advantages.	
	A golden mind stoops not to shows of dross[5];	20
	I'll then nor give nor hazard aught[6] for lead.	

FACT FILE

Queen Elizabeth I (sometimes called **The Virgin Queen**) was often the object of similar wooing before she decided to be married to England.

TIP

Dating shows present their candidates in a particularly favourable light. To prove their eligibility these people have to pass tests similar to Task 4.

TIP

Shakespeare's rhythm Before acting out the scene in Task 5, you may want to consult the rules about Shakespeare's rhythm on p. 111 again.

[1] **casket** small box
[2] **blunt** *(here)* direct
[3] **hazard** risk
[4] **to survey** to read closely
[5] **dross** sth with little value
[6] **aught** *(arch)* anything

117

6 The Merchant of Venice

What says the silver with her virgin hue[7]?
"Who chooseth me, shall get as much as he deserves."
As much as he deserves – pause then, Morocco,
And weigh thy value with an even[8] hand. 25
If thou be'st rated by thy estimation
Thou dost deserve enough; and yet enough
May not extend[9] so far as to the lady;
And yet to be afeared of my deserving
Were but a weak disabling[10] of myself. 30
As much as I deserve: why, that's the lady.
I do in birth deserve her, and in fortunes,
In graces, and in qualities of breeding[11]:
But more than these, in love I do deserve.
What if I strayed[12] no farther, but chose here? 35
Let's see once more this saying graved in gold:
"Who chooseth me, shall gain what many men desire."
Why, that's the lady; all the world desires her.
From the four corners of the earth they come
To kiss this shrine[13], this mortal breathing saint. 40
The Hyrcanian deserts and the vasty wilds
Of wide Arabia are as throughfares[14] now
For princes to come view fair Portia.
The watery kingdom[15], whose ambitious head
Spits in the face of heaven, is no bar 45
To stop the foreign spirits, but they come
As o'er a brook[16] to see fair Portia.
One of these three contains her heavenly picture.
Is't like that lead contains her? 'Twere damnation
To think so base[17] a thought; it were too gross[18] 50
To rib her cerecloth[19] in the òbscure grave.
Or shall I think in silver she's immured,
Being ten times undervalued to tried gold[20]?
O sinful thought! Never so rich a gem
Was set in worse than gold. They have in England 55
A coin that bears the figure of an angel
Stampèd in gold; but that's insculped upon:
But here an angel in a golden bed
Lies all within. Deliver me the key:
Here do I choose, and thrive[21] I as I may. 60

Portia   There take it, prince, and if my form lie there,
Then I am yours.
(Morocco unlocks the gold casket)

Morocco   A carrion[22] death, within whose empty eye
There is a written scroll[23]. I'll read the writing.
   "All that glisters is not gold; 65
   Often have you heard that told.
   Many a man his life hath sold
   But my outside to behold.
   Gilded[24] tombs do worms infold.
   Had you been as wise as bold[25], 70
   Young in limbs, in judgement old,
   Your answer had not been inscrolled.
   Fare you well, your suit is cold."
Cold indeed, and labour lost;
Then farewell heat, and welcome frost. 75
Portia, adieu, I have too grieved[26] a heart
To take a tedious[27] leave: thus losers part.
(Exit Morocco with his train)

Portia   A gentle riddance! Draw the curtains, go.
Let all of his complexion[28] choose me so.   *(Exeunt)*   II, 7, 1–79

[7] **hue** shine, shade of colour
[8] **even** *(here)* balanced
[9] **to extend** to reach
[10] **disabling** thinking too little of oneself
[11] **qualities of breeding** behaviour, manners
[12] **to stray** *(here)* to search
[13] **shrine** place of worship and rememb-rance
[14] **throughfare** wide open road
[15] **watery kingdom** oceans, the sea
[16] **brook** small river
[17] **base** low
[18] **gross** unacceptable
[19] **cerecloth** cloth in which a corpse is buried
[20] **tried gold** gold made pure
[21] **to thrive** to do well
[22] **carrion** skull
[23] **scroll** textroll
[24] **gilded** covered with a layer of gold
[25] **bold** courageous
[26] **grieved** sad
[27] **tedious** long
[28] **complexion** colour of skin

The Merchant of Venice | 6

5 Figures of speech

First focus

1 *With the help of the plot outline (Act 2, ll. 8–15) describe what has happened to Shylock so far.*

_____

_____

2 *Find examples of repetition, exclamation, parallelism, contrast and onomatopoeia in this short text and explain which effect they have on you.*

Stylistic device	Example	Effect
repetition		
exclamation		
parallelism		
contrast		
onomatopoeia		

> **TIP**
>
> **repetition:** reappearance of the same or similar linguistic elements
> **exclamation:** an outcry
> **parallelism:** textual elements organised in a parallel structure
> **contrast:** putting two extremes into opposition, cf. **Green Line Oberstufe Niedersachsen** p. 296
> **onomatopoeia:** words that through their pronunciation describe a sound

3 *Assess Shylock's character development with regard to compassion, empathy with Jessica, mercy or pardon.*

_____

_____

_____

_____

Second focus

4 [👥] ***Discussion:*** *With your partner discuss Shylock's situation considering the above mentioned aspects of compassion, empathy, mercy and pardon. One of you sympathises with Shylock whereas the other vehemently disagrees. Write down your respective arguments and present your discussion about Shylock's situation in class.* →S26

_____

_____

_____

5 ***Writing:*** *Create an additional aside for Jessica in which she tries to win the audience's favour by claiming that under certain circumstances it is even legitimate to ruin your father by taking a big part of his estate.* →S15

Solanio	I never heard a passion[1] so confused,
	So strange, outrageous[2], and so variable,
	As the dog Jew did utter[3] in the streets:
	"My daughter! O my ducats! O my daughter! 15
	Fled with a Christian! O my Christian ducats!
	Justice! The law! My ducats and my daughter!
	A sealèd bag, two sealèd bags of ducats,
	Of double ducats, stolen from me by my daughter!
	And jewels – two stones, two rich and precious stones, 20
	Stolen by my daughter! Justice! Find the girl!
	She hath the stones upon her and the ducats!"
	II, 8, 12–22

[1] **passion** passionate outburst
[2] **outrageous** shocking
[3] **to utter** to produce a sound

6 The Merchant of Venice

6 Creating atmosphere

First focus

1 *Read the text and explain the atmosphere the metaphors in lines 91–93 create.*
   _____
   _____

2 *Describe in your own words the image of Bassanio that is alluded to indirectly.*
   _____
   _____

3 *For a personal profile in a celebrity magazine you are asked to hand in a short portrait of a present-day Bassanio. Include a picture to illustrate your choice.* →S10

   Personal profile:
   _____
   _____
   _____

Second focus

4 a) *Using this scene as a starting point, write a short portfolio of this present-day celebrity for a partnership agency. Include three metaphors of your own choice.*
   _____
   _____
   _____
   _____

b) **Presentation:** *Present your client in a thirty-second ad for an upcoming dating-show on a commercial TV channel.*

■ **In the meantime:** Bassanio is about to arrive at Belmont, thus drawing together two important threads of the plot. This scene comes directly after the unsuccessful visit of the Prince of Arragon in his attempt to win Portia (cf. plot outline, Act II, ll. 16–18).

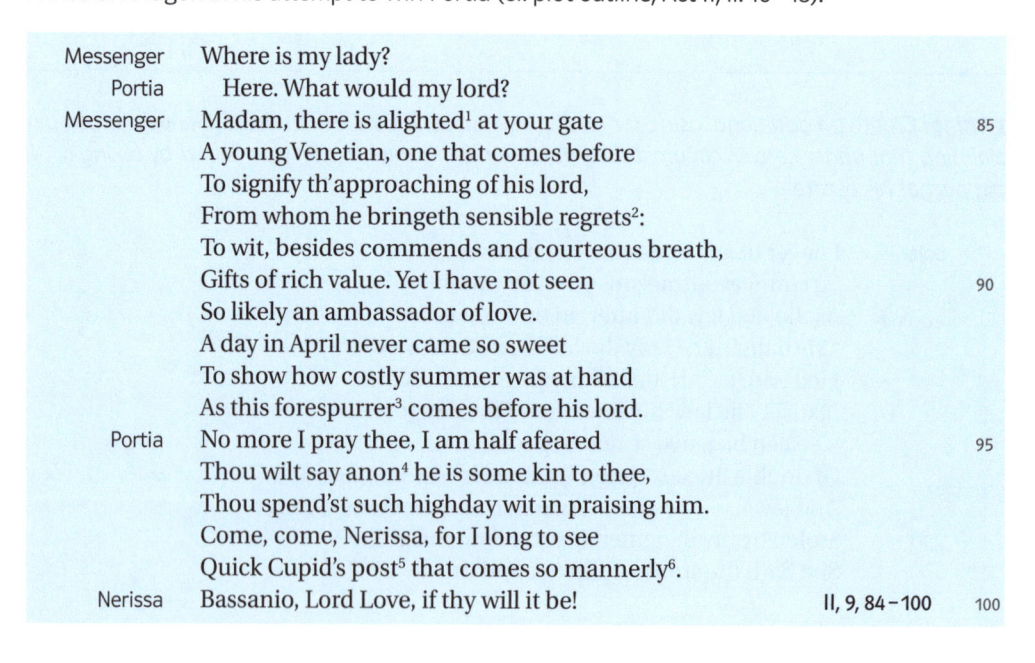

Messenger	Where is my lady?	
Portia	Here. What would my lord?	
Messenger	Madam, there is alighted[1] at your gate	85
	A young Venetian, one that comes before	
	To signify th'approaching of his lord,	
	From whom he bringeth sensible regrets[2]:	
	To wit, besides commends and courteous breath,	
	Gifts of rich value. Yet I have not seen	90
	So likely an ambassador of love.	
	A day in April never came so sweet	
	To show how costly summer was at hand	
	As this forespurrer[3] comes before his lord.	
Portia	No more I pray thee, I am half afeared	95
	Thou wilt say anon[4] he is some kin to thee,	
	Thou spend'st such highday wit in praising him.	
	Come, come, Nerissa, for I long to see	
	Quick Cupid's post[5] that comes so mannerly[6].	
Nerissa	Bassanio, Lord Love, if thy will it be!	

II, 9, 84–100   100

[1] **to alight** to get out of a vehicle
[2] **regrets** *(here)* presents
[3] **forespurrer** horseman who goes before others
[4] **anon** very soon
[5] **Cupid's post** messenger of the God of love
[6] **mannerly** in an attractive way

The Merchant of Venice | 6

7 Stylistic devices

First focus

1 a) *How did the Venetian Christians treat Shylock? In the table make a list in your own words (ll. 19–45).*
b) *On the right in the table, note down the similarities between Christians and Jews (ll. 46–57).*

Treatment by the Venetian Christians	Similarities between Christians and Jews
_____	_____
_____	_____
_____	_____
_____	_____
_____	_____
_____	_____
_____	_____

2 *Find three stylistic devices in Shylock's speech that appeal to you most and explain why this is so.*

1. _____
2. _____
3. _____

3 *Explore Shylock's alternative to the concept of revenge (l. 57).*

_____
_____
_____

Second focus

4 [👥] *Reacting in different ways to your opponent helps you make your point more clearly.*
a) *Practical exercises:*
1. *One half of the class recites Shylock's soliloquy facing the other half, which has to react with some mimed responses (ll. 42–57).*
2. *This time the responding group answers in an aggressive mood to Shylock's protest.*
3. *Repeat the exercise. This time the answering group tries to pacify Shylock with de-escalating responses.*
   In between the different stages of the exercise groups may be swapped and individual members are free to choose as much text as they wish.
b) *Discuss the effects of the different forms of presentation.* →S26

Solanio	How now, Shylock, what news among the merchants?	
Shylock	You knew, none so well, none so well as you, of my daughter's flight.	20
Salarino	That's certain; I for my part knew the tailor that made the wings she flew withal.	
Solanio	And Shylock for his own part knew the bird was fledged[1], and then it is the complexion[2] of them all to leave the dam[3].	25
Shylock	She is damned for it.	
Salarino	That's certain – if the devil may be her judge.	
Shylock	My own flesh and blood to rebel[4]!	
Solanio	Out upon it, old carrion! Rebels it at these years[5]?	
Shylock	I say my daughter is my flesh and my blood.	30

[1] **fledged** to become able to fly
[2] **complexion** general character of sth or sb
[3] **dam** mother bird
[4] **to rebel** to refuse to follow
[5] **rebels it at these years** can't you get an erection?

6 | The Merchant of Venice

Salarino	There is more difference between thy flesh and hers than between jet and ivory; more between your bloods than there is between red wine and Rhenish. But tell us, do you hear whether Antonio have had any loss at sea or no?
Shylock	There I have another bad match: a bankrupt, a prodigal⁶, who dare scarce⁷ show his head on the Rialto, a beggar that was used to come so smug upon the mart⁸. Let him look to his bond. He was wont⁹ to call me usurer; let him look to his bond. He was wont to lend money for Christian courtesy; let him look to his bond.
Salarino	Why, I am sure if he forfeit thou wilt not take his flesh. What's that good for?
Shylock	To bait¹⁰ fish withal; if it will feed nothing else, it will feed my revenge. He hath disgraced me, and hindered me half a million, laughed at my losses, mocked at my gains, scorned my nation, thwarted my bargains, cooled my friends, heated mine enemies – and what's his reason? I am a Jew. Hath not a Jew eyes? Hath not a Jew hands, organs, dimensions, senses, affections, passions? Fed with the same food, hurt with the same weapons, subject to the same diseases, healed by the same means, warmed and cooled by the same winter and summer as a Christian is? If you prick¹¹ us, do we not bleed? If you tickle us, do we not laugh? If you poison us, do we not die? And if you wrong us, shall we not revenge? If we are like you in the rest, we will resemble you in that. If a Jew wrong¹² a Christian, what is his humility¹³? Revenge. If a Christian wrong a Jew, what should his sufferance¹⁴ be by Christian example? Why, revenge! The villainy you teach me I will execute¹⁵, and it shall go hard but I will better the instruction¹⁶.

III, 1, 19–57

⁶ **prodigal** wasteful person
⁷ **scarce** hardly to be seen
⁸ **mart** market
⁹ **wont** usual behaviour of a person
¹⁰ **to bait** to put a small piece of food on a hook to catch fish
¹¹ **prick** cut, make a small hole
¹² **to wrong** to treat so unfairly
¹³ **humility** *(here)* expected kindness, acceptance
¹⁴ **sufferance** *Duldsamkeit*
¹⁵ **to execute** to practice
¹⁶ **to better the instruction** to do sth better than the original

8 Rising conflict (Preparing a solution)

First focus

1 *Determine the amount of gold/money which Portia will equip Bassanio with to "deface the bond".*

2 *Explain Portia's plan for the near future as well as the pun in line 312.*

3 **Writing:** *Capital punishment because of 3000 ducats? Gratiano, a friend of Antonio's, publishes a pamphlet reflecting on Antonio's and Bassanio's situation in a religious context.* →S14

The Merchant of Venice | 6

Second focus

4 *Explore the effects a choral reading of the letter has on you when it is read out in different ways:* a neutral tone • agonised • in a loving way • in a patronising way. →S26

■ **In the meantime:** Shylock has had Antonio arrested. Meanwhile at Belmont, Bassanio has won Portia in the lottery of the caskets. Likewise Gratiano asks Portia and Bassanio to let him marry Nerissa. A letter from Antonio informs the company about his deplorable fate. Portia enquires about the details of the letter (cf. plot outline, Act III, ll. 1–12).

Portia	What sums owes he the Jew?	
Bassanio	For me, three thousand ducats.	
Portia	What, no more?	
	Pay him six thousand, and deface¹ the bond.	
	Double six thousand and then treble that,	
	Before a friend of this description	300
	Shall lose a hair through Bassanio's fault.	
	First go with me to church, and call me wife,	
	And then away to Venice to your friend!	
	For never shall you lie by Portia's side	
	With an unquiet soul. You shall have gold	305
	To pay the petty² debt twenty times over.	
	When it is paid, bring your true friend along.	
	My maid Nerissa and myself meantime	
	Will live as maids and widows. Come away,	
	For you shall hence³ upon your wedding day.	310
	Bid your friends welcome, show a merry cheer;	
	Since you are dear bought, I will love you dear.	
	But let me hear the letter of your friend.	
Bassanio	*(Reads)* "Sweet Bassanio, my ships have all miscarried, my creditors grow cruel, my estate is very low; my bond to the Jew is forfeit,	315
	and since in paying it, it is impossible I should live, all debts are cleared between you and I if I might but see you at my death. Notwithstanding⁴, use your pleasure; if your love do not persuade you to come, let not my letter."	
Portia	O love! Dispatch⁵ all business and be gone.	320
Bassanio	Since I have your good leave to go away,	
	I will make haste. But till I come again	
	No bed shall e'er be guilty of my stay	
	Nor rest be interposer 'twixt⁶ us twain⁷.	III, 2, 296–324

TIP

Choral reading: Rehearsing lines in a group prepares everyone for individual contributions. Personal movement and gestures as well as sound effects and music may be used to intensify the performance of the ideas you develop.

¹ **to deface** to make sth unvalid by writing on it
² **petty** unimportant, negligeable
³ **to hence** *(here)* to depart
⁴ **notwithstanding** despite this situation
⁵ **to dispatch** *(here)* to finish
⁶ **twixt** between
⁷ **twain** *(arch)* two

9 Development of the conflict

First focus

1 *Read the text and explain Antonio's change of mind from line 3 to line 19.*

_____
_____
_____
_____

2 *Examine the consequences as laid down in lines 20–31.*

_____
_____
_____
_____

TIP

Working with the text: Mark relevant aspects of the text before working out the answers. For Tasks 3–6 use a different colour for each task.

6 The Merchant of Venice

TIP

How to create a rap with an echo: Divide Shylock's lines into parts and add a chorus answering each of the statements with a monotonous "I'll have my bond", e.g.
I'll have my bond
Speak not against my bond
I'll have my bond
I have sworn an oath
I'll have my bond
etc.

Second focus

3 *Develop different reactions to visualise Antonio's various states of mind in lines 4–11 and line 19.*

4 a) *Rearrange Shylock's lines (ll. 4–10) to make it a rap. For this you could echo each statement with "I'll have my bond". Perform it.* →S6
   b) *Choose a different response for lines 12–17.*

_____
_____
_____
_____
_____

5 [👥] *In a different version of lines 4–17 Antonio and Shylock meet again. For this version the class is divided into two lines opposing each other. Everyone in class takes over one line of his character. Pair after pair walks towards their respective partner, addressing each other in either a superior or an inferior way.*

6 a) [👥] *One of you takes on the part of Antonio, trying to persuade Shylock to change his mind, while the other blocks off any form of communication with monotonous answers. Mark suitable phrases from the text and use them.*
   b) *Explain how you felt acting out your part during the task.*

Shylock	Jailer, look to him. Tell not me of mercy.
	This is the fool that lent out money gratis.
	Jailer, look to him.
Antonio	Hear me yet, good Shylock –
Shylock	I'll have my bond, speak not against my bond;
	I have sworn an oath that I will have my bond. 5
	Thou call'st me dog before thou hadst a cause
	But since I am a dog, beware my fangs¹.
	The Duke shall grant me justice. I do wonder,
	Thou naughty² jailer, that thou art so fond
	To come abroad with him at his request. 10
Antonio	I pray thee hear me speak –
Shylock	I'll have my bond; I will not hear thee speak;
	I'll have my bond, and therefore speak no more.
	I'll not be made a soft and dull-eyed fool,
	To shake the head, relent³, and sigh, and yield⁴ 15
	To Christian intercessors⁵. Follow not!
	I'll have no speaking. I will have my bond. *(Exit)*
Solanio	It is the most impenetrable⁶ cur
	That ever kept with⁷ men.
Antonio	Let him alone.
	I'll follow him no more with bootless⁸ prayers. 20
	He seeks my life, his reason well I know:
	I oft delivered from his forfeitures
	Many that have at times made moan to me
	Therefore he hates me.
Solanio	I am sure the Duke
	Will never grant this forfeiture to hold. 25
Antonio	The Duke cannot deny the course of law;
	For the commodity⁹ that strangers have
	With us in Venice, if it be denied,
	Will much impeach¹⁰ the justice of the state,
	Since that the trade and profit of the city 30
	Consisteth of all nations. Therefore go.

III, 3, 1–31

¹ **fangs** teeth
² **naughty** behaving badly
³ **to relent** to allow reluctantly
⁴ **to yield** to give in
⁵ **intercessor** person who uses influence to make authorities change their minds
⁶ **impenetrable** which cannot be seen or gone through
⁷ **kept with** lived with
⁸ **bootless** hopeless
⁹ **commodity** *(here)* trade
¹⁰ **to impeach** *(here)* to damage the reputation

The Merchant of Venice | 6

10 The trial begins

First focus

1 a) *State in detail how the Duke describes Shylock's behaviour so far. Note down keywords and the lines they appear in.*

Former behaviour	Future conduct
_____	_____
_____	_____
_____	_____

b) *Contrast his observations with his expectations of Shylock's future conduct.*

_____
_____
_____

2 a) *Shylock makes a threat and asks two rhetorical questions.*

threat: _____

rhetorical questions: _____
_____

b) *Write down an answer to the rhetorical questions.*

_____
_____

c) *Based on this answer design a (legal) counter attack taking his reasoning seriously.*

_____
_____
_____
_____

Second focus

3 *Write detailed stage directions for how to act out each single idea of the extract. Perform the scene accordingly. Write down your ideas on the copy provided by your teacher.*

4 *Write a screenplay anticipating different camera positions, shots and angles taking into account the different expressions of the speakers. Verify your decisions by comparing them with a film production of the play of your choice.*

> (Enter SHYLOCK)
> Duke Make room and let him stand before our face.
> Shylock, the world thinks, and I think so too,
> That thou but leadest this fashion of thy malice[1]
> To the last hour of act, and then 'tis thought
> Thou'lt show thy mercy and remorse[2] more strange   20
> Than is thy strange apparent cruelty.
> And where thou now exacts the penalty,
> Which is a pound of this poor merchant's flesh,
> Thou wilt not only loose the forfeiture

TIP

Use the copy of **Extract 10** your teacher will give you for your stage directions.

TIP

For this task refer to the special skill on the visual aspects of film that your teacher will give you.

[1] **malice** evil intent
[2] **remorse** bad feeling about an action

6 The Merchant of Venice

	But, touched with human gentleness and love,	25
	Forgive a moiety³ of the principal,	
	Glancing an eye of pity on his losses	
	That have of late so huddled⁴ on his back,	
	Enow⁵ to press a royal merchant down	
	And pluck⁶ commiseration of his state	30
	From brassy⁷ bosoms and rough hearts of flint⁸,	
	From stubborn Turks, and Tartars never trained	
	To offices of tender courtesy.	
	We all expect a gentle answer, Jew.	
Shylock	I have possessed your grace of what I purpose,	35
	And by our holy Sabaoth have I sworn	
	To have the due and forfeit of my bond.	
	If you deny it, let the danger light	
	Upon your charter and your city's freedom!	
	You'll ask me why I rather choose to have	40
	A weight of carrion flesh than to receive	
	Three thousand ducats. I'll not answer that –	
	But say it is my humour⁹: is it answered?	
	What if my house be troubled with¹⁰ a rat,	
	And I be pleased to give ten thousand ducats	45
	To have it baned¹¹? What, are you answered yet?	

IV, 1, 16 – 46

³ **moiety** small portion
⁴ **huddled** massed together
⁵ **enow** enough
⁶ **to pluck** to pull with quick movement
⁷ **brassy** *(here)* harsh
⁸ **flint** stone
⁹ **humour** mood
¹⁰ **troubled with** suffering from
¹¹ **baned** killed by poison

11 Shylock reinforces his view

First focus

1 *Calculate how many ducats Shylock refuses as compensation:* _____ ducats

2 a) *Vocabulary:* Find out the differences between the terms "legal" and "legitimate".

legal	legitimate

b) *Discuss whether Shylock's legally correct claims are morally legitimate.*
_____
_____

3 *Assess Shylock's argumentation in a comment based on the articles of the United Nation's Declaration of Human Rights on the opposite page. Write about 150 words.* → S14, → S22

The Merchant of Venice | 6

Second focus

4 *Present your comment as a newsflash contribution for a TV or radio programme.* →S17

■ **In the meantime:** At the end of Act III Portia and Nerissa have set out for Venice disguised as a lawyer and his clerk to defend Antonio in court. To achieve this, Portia has sent a messenger to the lawyer who was originally asked to help Antonio. In this letter she wants him to excuse himself for not being able to come and to provide her with a legally sound strategy to rescue Antonio. This will allow her to wear a disguise and take on the task of saving Antonio herself (cf. plot outline, Act IV ll. 4–8).

> **TIP**
>
> A **newsflash** is an important piece of news that makes media interrupt their broadcast. The announcement needs to be concise to create immediate attention.

Antonio	Therefore I do beseech you	80
	Make no moe¹ offers, use no farther means,	
	But with all brief and plain conveniency²	
	Let me have judgement, and the Jew his will.	
Bassanio	For thy three thousand ducats here is six.	
Shylock	If every ducat in six thousand ducats	85
	Were in six parts, and every part a ducat,	
	I would not draw them; I would have my bond.	
Duke	How shalt thou hope for mercy, rendering³ none?	
Shylock	What judgement shall I dread, doing no wrong?	
	You have among you many a purchased slave,	90
	Which, like your asses and your dogs and mules,	
	You use in abject⁴ and in slavish parts	
	Because you bought them. Shall I say to you,	
	'Let them be free! Marry them to your heirs⁵!	
	Why sweat they under burdens? Let their beds	95
	Be made as soft as yours, and let their palates⁶	
	Be seasoned with such viands⁷'? You will answer,	
	"The slaves are ours." So do I answer you.	
	The pound of flesh which I demand of him	
	Is dearly bought; 'tis mine, and I will have it.	100
	If you deny me, fie upon⁸ your law:	
	There is no force in the decrees⁹ of Venice.	
	I stand for judgement. Answer: shall I have it?	IV, 1, 80–103

¹ **moe** more
² **conveniency** suitability; matter of factness
³ **rendering** giving, conceding
⁴ **abject** contemptuous
⁵ **heirs** people who receive your possessions upon your death
⁶ **palates** Gaumen *(lat. palatum)*
⁷ **viands** food
⁸ **fie upon** shame on
⁹ **decree** official order

EXCERPT FROM THE UNIVERSAL DECLARATION OF HUMAN RIGHTS
(adopted by the United Nations on December 10, 1948)

THE GENERAL ASSEMBLY PROCLAIMS THIS UNIVERSAL DECLARATION OF HUMAN RIGHTS as a common standard of achievement for all peoples and all nations, to the end that every individual and every organ of society, keeping this Declaration constantly in mind, shall strive by teaching and education to promote respect for these rights and freedoms and by progressive measures, national and international, to secure their universal and effective recognition and observance, both among the peoples of Member States themselves and among the peoples of territories under their jurisdiction.

Article 1
All human beings are born free and equal in dignity and rights. They are endowed with reason and conscience and should act towards one another in a spirit of brotherhood.

Article 2
Everyone is entitled to all the rights and freedoms set forth in this Declaration, without distinction of any kind, such as race, colour, sex, language, religion, political or other opinion, national or social origin, property, birth or other status. Furthermore, no distinction shall be made on the basis of the political, jurisdictional or international status of the country or territory to which a person belongs, whether it be independent, trust, non-self-governing or under any other limitation of sovereignty.

6 The Merchant of Venice

12 Refutation on different moral grounds

First focus

1 **Pre-reading discussion:** *A man cannot pay for medical treatment for his fatally ill child. He steals money to pay for the necessary medication and is consequently prosecuted.*
   a) *You are asked to assess this case taking into consideration the following values:*
      THOU SHALT NOT STEAL!

   _____
   _____

   b) *Establish a personal ranking for the values for this case adding further principles of your choice if necessary.* →S26

   ☐ responsibility   ☐ justice   ☐ mercy   ☐ _____
   ☐ obedience to the law ☐ compassion   ☐ the 7th commandment ☐ _____

2 *Define the term "mercy" by looking at its general quality (ll. 180–183). Mark the concept in the text and explain it in your own words.*

   _____
   _____

3 *Explain why the principle of mercy makes kings similar to God in one way (ll. 184–193).*

   _____
   _____
   _____

4 *Discuss Portia's and Shylock's ways of seeking salvation (ll. 194–198).*

   _____
   _____
   _____
   _____

5 *Comment on Bassanio's suggestion that one evil should be replaced with another and on Portia's answer.* →S14

   _____
   _____
   _____
   _____

Second focus

> **TIP**
>
> Use the handout your teacher will give you to prepare the stage directions you need to put on the copy of **Extract 12**.

6 *Imagine you the director's assistant for a production at the Globe Theatre. In her speech Portia addresses four parties: Shylock, Antonio and his train, the Duke and the theatre audience. Write stage directions on a handout from your teacher advising the speaker:*
   - *how to use her hand when addressing the four groups,*
   - *where to position herself among the groups,*
   - *which lines to direct at the respective groups.* →S4

The Merchant of Venice — 6

7 *Try out your ideas. Three speakers prepare the speech according to your stage directions. They may add their personal touches. Perform the scene. Exchange the different impressions the three performances have on you.* → S7

Portia	Is your name Shylock?
Shylock	Shylock is my name.
Portia	Of a strange nature is the suit[1] you follow,
	Yet in such rule that the Venetian law
	Cannot impugn[2] you as you do proceed. 175
	– You stand within his danger, do you not?
Antonio	Ay, so he says.
Portia	Do you confess[3] the bond?
Antonio	I do.
Portia	Then must the Jew be merciful.
Shylock	On what compulsion must I? Tell me that.
Portia	The quality of mercy is not strained[4], 180
	It droppeth as the gentle rain from heaven
	Upon the place beneath. It is twice blest[5]:
	It blesseth him that gives, and him that takes.
	'Tis mightiest in the mightiest, it becomes[6]
	The thronèd monarch better than his crown. 185
	His sceptre shows the force of temporal power,
	The attribute to awe[7] and majesty,
	Wherein doth sit the dread and fear of kings;
	But mercy is above this sceptred sway[8].
	It is enthronèd in the hearts of kings, 190
	It is an attribute to God himself,
	And earthly power doth then show likest God's
	When mercy seasons[9] justice. Therefore, Jew,
	Though justice be thy plea, consider this:
	That in the course of justice, none of us 195
	Should see salvation. We do pray for mercy,
	And that same prayer doth teach us all to render
	The deeds of mercy. I have spoke thus much
	To mitigate[10] the justice of thy plea,
	Which if thou follow, this strict court of Venice 200
	Must needs give sentence 'gainst the merchant there.
Shylock	My deeds upon my head! I crave[11] the law,
	The penalty and forfeit of my bond.
Portia	Is he not able to discharge the money?
Bassanio	Yes, here I tender it for him in the court, 205
	Yea, twice the sum; if that will not suffice[12],
	I will be bound to pay it ten times o'er
	On forfeit of my hands, my head, my heart.
	If this will not suffice, it must appear
	That malice bears down truth. And I beseech you[13] 210
	Wrest[14] once the law to your authority;
	To do a great right, do a little wrong,
	And curb[15] this cruel devil of his will.
Portia	It must not be; there is no power in Venice
	Can alter a decree establishèd 215
	'Twill be recorded for a precedent[16],
	And many an error by the same example
	Will rush into the state: it cannot be.

IV, 1, 172–218

[1] **suit** court case
[2] **to impugn** to raise doubts about sb character
[3] **to confess** to admit
[4] **not strained** cannot be forced
[5] **blest** given blessing by God
[6] **to become**s to look good upon
[7] **awe** fear
[8] **sway** influence, control
[9] **to season** to give spices, taste to sth
[10] **to mitigate** to make sth less serious; "mitigating circumstances"
[11] **to crave** to long for
[12] **to suffice** to be enough
[13] **to beseech** to beg strongly
[14] **to wrest** to take away violently
[15] **to curb** to keep sb from exacting sth
[16] **precedent** first case, example

6 The Merchant of Venice

13 Is Shylock about to succeed?

First focus

1 Review what you have found out about Shylock's character and contrast it with the image presented in this extract.

Former findings	Image in the extract

2 Explain which music or sound effects you would choose to accompany this scene in a theatre and for a film production.

Theatre production	Film production

Second focus

3 Portia appears to be interested in the continuation of the legal proceedings but is not personally involved. Shylock, in contrast, gets increasingly keen. Perform the scene.

Portia	Why then, thus it is:	240
	You must prepare your bosom[1] for his knife.	
Shylock	O noble judge, O excellent young man!	
Portia	For the intent[2] and purpose of the law	
	Hath full relation to the penalty	
	Which here appeareth due upon the bond.	245
Shylock	'Tis very true. O wise and upright judge.	
	How much more elder art thou than thy looks!	
Portia	Therefore lay bare your bosom.	
Shylock	Ay, his breast.	
	So says the bond, doth it not, noble judge?	
	'Nearest his heart': those are the very words.	250
Portia	It is so. Are there balance[3] here to weigh	
	The flesh?	
Shylock	I have them ready.	
Portia	Have by some surgeon[4], Shylock, on your charge,	
	To stop his wounds, lest[5] he do bleed to death.	
Shylock	Is it so nominated in the bond?	255
Portia	It is not so expressed, but what of that?	
	'Twere good you do so much for charity.	
Shylock	I cannot find it, 'tis not in the bond.	IV, 1, 240–258

[1] **bosom** breast
[2] **intent** aim
[3] **balance** weights
[4] **surgeon** doctor
[5] **lest** so that he doesn't bleed to death

The Merchant of Venice | 6

14 Shylock defeated

First focus

1 *Antonio does not say a word in Extract 13 even though his life is at stake. He merely follows Portia's and Shylock's negotiations concerning his life, during which he goes through different stages of emotion. How does Antonio feel? Find five words from the word field "fear" and match them with statements by Portia and Shylock from the two excerpts. (Extract 13, ll. 240–255; Extract 14, ll. 295–300).* →S10

Antonio's feelings	Portia	Line	Shylock	Line
fear	prepare your bosom	241	O noble judge	242

2 a) *Continue the table now concentrating on Antonio's reactions.*

Name	Line	Quote	Antonio's feelings
Portia	301f. 312		
Shylock	314		
Portia	320		
Gratiano	330		
Portia	335 339		
Shylock	342		
Portia	359		

b) *Follow Antonio's changes of emotion in the lines above and report the individual steps in a newsflash.*

Second focus

3 [👥] **Tableaux:** *Divide the class into groups of three or more. Below are a number of passages from the extract. Each group chooses a passage and presents its contents as a freeze frame. Position the individual frames one after the other to create a picture story. Every group member takes a part in the groups frame. You could take photographs of the frames and produce a picture story yourself.*

TIP

A **newsflash** is an important piece of news that makes media interrupt their broadcast. The announcement needs to be concise to create immediate attention.

Text 1: ll. 295–297   Text 2: ll. 298–300   Text 3: ll. 301–309   Text 4: ll. 309–312
Text 5: ll. 313–318   Text 6: ll. 319–330   Text 7: ll. 331–333   Text 8: ll. 334–338
Text 9: ll. 339–342   Text 10: ll. 243-359

Portia	A pound of that same merchant's flesh is thine, The court awards it, and the law does give it.	295
Shylock	Most rightful judge!	
Portia	And you must cut this flesh from off his breast; The law allows it, and the court awards it.	
Shylock	Most learned judge! A sentence: come, prepare.	300
Portia	Tarry¹ a little, there is something else. This bond doth give thee here no jot² of blood.	

¹ **to tarry** to wait
² **jot** very small quantity

The Merchant of Venice

	The words expressly are 'a pound of flesh'.
	Take then thy bond, take thou thy pound of flesh,
	But in the cutting it, if thou dost shed 305
	One drop of Christian blood, thy lands and goods
	Are by the laws of Venice confiscate
	Unto the state of Venice.
Gratiano	O upright judge!
	Mark, Jew – O learned judge!
Shylock	Is that the law?
Portia	Thyself³ shall see the Act. 310
	For as thou urgest⁴ justice, be assured
	Thou shalt have justice more than thou desirest.
Gratiano	O learned judge! Mark, Jew: a learned judge.
Shylock	I take this offer then. Pay the bond thrice
	And let the Christian go.
Bassanio	Here is the money. 315
Portia	Soft.⁵
	The Jew shall have all justice; soft, no haste;
	He shall have nothing but the penalty.
Gratiano	O Jew, an upright judge, a learned judge!
Portia	Therefore prepare thee to cut off the flesh. 320
	Shed thou no blood, nor cut thou less nor more
	But just a pound of flesh. If thou tak'st more
	Or less than a just pound, be it but so much
	As makes it light or heavy in the substance
	Or the division of the twentieth part 325
	Of one poor scruple⁶ – nay, if the scale do turn
	But in the estimation of a hair,
	Thou diest, and all thy goods are confiscate.
Gratiano	A second Daniel; a Daniel, Jew!
	Now, infidel, I have you on the hip.⁷ 330
Portia	Why doth the Jew pause? Take thy forfeiture.
Shylock	Give me my principal⁸, and let me go.
Bassanio	I have it ready for thee; here it is.
Portia	He hath refused it in the open court.
	He shall have merely justice and his bond. 335
Gratiano	A Daniel, still say I, a second Daniel!
	I thank thee, Jew, for teaching me that word.
Shylock	Shall I not have barely my principal?
Portia	Thou shalt have nothing but the forfeiture,
	To be so taken at thy peril⁹, Jew. 340
Shylock	Why then, the devil give him good of it!
Portia	I'll stay no longer question.
	Tarry, Jew:
	The law hath yet another hold on you.
	It is enacted in the laws of Venice,
	If it be proved against an alien 345
	That by direct or indirect attempts
	He seek the life of any citizen,
	The party 'gainst the which he doth contrive¹⁰
	Shall seize one half his goods, the other half
	Comes to the privy coffer¹¹ of the state, 350
	And the offender's life lies in the mercy
	Of the Duke only, 'gainst all other voice.
	In which predicament¹² I say thou stand'st;
	For it appears by manifest¹³ proceeding
	That indirectly, and directly too, 355
	Thou hast contrived against the very life
	Of the defendant, and thou hast incurred
	The danger formerly by me rehearsed.
	Down, therefore, and beg mercy of the Duke. IV, 1, 295–359

³ **thyself** yourself
⁴ **to urge** to demand
⁵ **soft** stop
⁶ **scruple** weight; about 1.3 grams
⁷ **I have you on the hip** I have caught you now
⁸ **principal** the original sum
⁹ **at thy peril** at your own risk
¹⁰ **to contrive** to make plans against sb
¹¹ **privy coffer** money belonging to the community
¹² **predicament** problematic unpleasant situation
¹³ **manifest** shown clearly, openly

The Merchant of Venice | 6

15 Shylock's punishment

First focus

1 *Mark the punishment as described in the text and give a detailed account of the punishment which Shylock receives for attempting to kill a Venetian citizen.*

_____
_____
_____
_____
_____
_____
_____

2 a) *Explain in modern English how the characters react to Shylock's punishment.*

Antonio
_____
_____
_____

Portia
_____
_____
_____

Gratiano
_____
_____
_____

The Duke
_____
_____
_____

b) *What is your reaction? Prepare your statement for a short radio/TV comment.*

_____
_____
_____

3 *Discuss if Shylock's punishment is an act of Christian mercy.*

_____
_____
_____

4 *Comment on the question whether in his defeat Shylock shows new traits.*

_____
_____
_____
_____
_____

6 | The Merchant of Venice

Second focus

5 *Present your ideas on how to play Shylock's part in lines 389 ff.*

_____

_____

6 [👥👥👥] *Form a circle and put a chair in the middle to represent Shylock. Now throw lines of your choice from this scene at "him", expressing your feelings.*

TIP

Use the copy of **Extract 15** your teacher will give you for your changes in the text.

7 *Imagine that Shylock is not present in the scene. Make all necessary changes in the text to act the scene in a variety of different moods, e.g. the remaining characters are relieved; they feel triumphant about their victory; they mock Shylock's situation.*

Shylock	Nay, take my life and all, pardon not that:	370
	You take my house when you do take the prop[1]	
	That doth sustain my house; you take my life	
	When you do take the means whereby I live.	
Portia	What mercy can you render him, Antonio?	
Gratiano	A halter[2] gratis – nothing else, for God's sake.	375
Antonio	So please my lord the Duke and all the court	
	To quit the fine for one half of his goods,	
	I am content, so he will let me have	
	The other half in use, to render[3] it	
	Upon his death unto the gentleman	380
	That lately stole his daughter.	
	Two things provided more: that for this favour	
	He presently become a Christian;	
	The other, that he do record a gift,[4]	
	Here in the court, of all he dies possessed	385
	Unto his son Lorenzo and his daughter.	
Duke	He shall do this, or else I do recant[5]	
	The pardon that I late pronouncèd here.	
Portia	Art thou[6] contented, Jew? What dost thou say?	
Shylock	I am content.	
Portia	Clerk, draw a deed of gift.	390
Shylock	I pray you give me leave to go from hence;	
	I am not well. Send the deed after me	
	And I will sign it.	
Duke	Get thee gone, but do it.	
Gratiano	In christening shalt thou have two godfathers:[7]	
	Had I been judge, thou shouldst have had ten more,	395
	To bring thee to the gallows[8], not to the font[9].	
	(Exit [Shylock])	
Duke	Sir, I entreat you[10] home with me to dinner.	
Portia	I humbly[11] do desire your grace of pardon.	
	I must away this night toward Padua,	
	And it is meet[12] I presently set forth.	400
Duke	I am sorry that your leisure serves you not.	
	Antonio, gratify[13] this gentleman,	
	For in my mind you are much bound to him.	
	(Exit Duke and his train)	IV, 1, 370–403

[1] **prop** item to suppport sth
[2] **halter** *(here)* rope
[3] **to render** to give, hand over
[4] **gift** present
[5] **to recant** to recall, to take back
[6] **art thou** are you?
[7] **godfathers** Paten
[8] **gallows** place of execution
[9] **font** place of baptizement
[10] **I entreat you** I beg you
[11] **humbly** modestly
[12] **meet** fitting, suitable
[13] **to gratify** *(here)* to pay out

8 *Many productions have "The Merchant of Venice" finish at the end of Act 4. With the help of the plot outline (Act V, ll. 1–10) discuss the possible reasons as well as advantages or disadvantages.*

9 **Creative writing:** *The play "Romeo and Juliet" ends with these lines: "For never was a story of more woe than this of Juliet and her Romeo." In a similar fashion write an epilogue for Shylock and present it to the class.* → S12

The Merchant of Venice | 6

C More on the play

1 Mediation: Interview mit Norbert Kentrup

Doing research on Shakespeare's "The Merchant of Venice", the drama group of your English partner school has heard that a German actor was the first to perform the part of Shylock in the first production of the play at Shakespeare's Globe Theatre in London. They are interested in what it was like for him. Using the information below write about his experiences in around 250 words as a contribution to their drama group newsletter.

■ **Herr Kentrup, was war für Sie das Besondere an dieser Rolle?**

Jeder war schon mal Außenseiter, der Alien, der Gemobbte, zu dick, zu klein, zu laut, zu deutsch, zu fremd. Eine Rabbinerin sagte mir, hätte Shakespeare das Stück heute geschrieben, wäre Shylock vielleicht kein Jude, sondern ein Muslim. Vor
5 400 Jahren hat ein Mensch dieses Wissen über Ausgegrenzte, über Fremde und ihre widersprüchliche Haltung als Opfer, aber auch als Täter zusammengefasst und ihm im 3. Akt, 1. Szene die erste Rede für Menschenrechte geschrieben. *Hath not a Jew eyes?* Diese vielschichtige Figur nach 400 Jahren als erster Deutscher im wiedererrichteten Globe Theater in London spielen zu dürfen war ein Geschenk.

10 ■ **Welche Reaktionen haben Sie in England erfahren darüber, dass Sie als Deutscher ausgerechnet in diesem Stück den Juden spielten?**

Dadurch, dass der Jude Sam Wanamaker sich auf dem Totenbett wünschte, dass ich als deutscher Nichtjude diese Rolle spielte, war ich wahrscheinlich geschützt, aber es gab Diskussionen, Fragen und auch Kommentare in Zeitungen und Gesprächen.
15 Nach der Premiere (gab es) viel internationales Lob und Anerkennung, aber auch Kritik.

■ **Wie haben Ihre Kollegen vom Globe Ihre Interpretation wertgeschätzt?**

Das war widersprüchlich, positiv und negativ. Es gab eine Menge an Kontroversen während der Proben. Mark Rylance, dem Theaterdirektor und Darsteller des
20 Bassanio, und Richard Olivier, dem Regisseur, bin ich sehr dankbar, dass sie dieses Risiko mit mir eingingen, denn ich hatte erst ein Jahr vorher angefangen, überhaupt Englisch zu lernen. (In der Schule nicht aufgepasst.) Mein Akzent war für englische Ohren bestimmt sehr fremd, was allerdings ja auch Sams Idee war. Es war ein multikulti Cast mit einem Inder, Chinesen, Afrikaner, Deutschen,
25 Italiener, Schweizerin etc. Verschiedene Theaterkulturen und Arbeitsweisen prallten aufeinander. Die englischen Kollegen spielen durch die in England übliche knappe Probenzeit mehr einen Charakter, der in allen Szenen ähnlich ist. Wir arbeiten in Deutschland konzeptioneller und die Figuren sind brüchiger, denn die Probenzeiten sind länger. Ich untersuche jeden Vers auf einen möglichen
30 Emotionswechsel, in jeder Szene versuche ich einen anderen Teil der Figur zu entdecken,
So spielte ich in jeder Szene einen anderen Teil des Shylock. Im 1. Akt den kosmopolitischen, witzigen, großzügigen Friedensstifter, der spontan einen Witz macht, wenn er die Wette mit dem Pfund Fleisch vorschlägt.
35 Meine Interpretation passte wenig zu dem Shylock-Bild, das einige in der Produktion hatten. Im 2. Akt, 2. Szene den dogmatischen fanatischen Orthodoxen, der seiner Tochter und seinem Diener die Hölle bereitet. Im 3. Akt, 1. Szene die verletzte aufjaulende Kreatur, die auf dem Marktplatz die Menschenrechte für sich reklamiert. Dann in der folgenden Szene mit Tubal den uneinsichtigen
40 dogmatischen Vater, der seine Tochter für tot erklärt. Im 3. Akt, 3. Szene den Rächer, und schließlich den vor Wut blinden, der in den 4. Akt geht, wissend, er wird verlieren, aber einmal Recht haben will: *The villainy you teach me I will execute ...* Die unterschiedlichen Ansichten und Spielweisen eskalierten bei meiner Darstellung im 4. Akt, wenn Shylock sagt: *I am content*. Sie wollten, dass ich das
45 spiele, was ich sage, demütig und geschlagen und gehe als Bekehrter ab. Ich wollte spielen, ich sage das, weil ich gezwungen werde, aber tue das Gegenteil und ziehe mir meinen jüdischen Gebetsschal über und gehe als aufrechter Jude ab.

6 The Merchant of Venice

> ■ **Könnten Sie diese Interpretation des Shylock in gleicher Weise auch in einer deutschen Produktion so umsetzen?**
>
> 50 Nein, denn in Deutschland ist man durch die furchtbare Vergangenheit vermeintlich politisch korrekter.
>
> ■ **Welche Gedanken können Sie deutschen Schülerinnen und Schülern nahelegen, wenn sie Shylock im Klassenzimmer darstellen? Welche Texte / Szenen bieten sich besonders gut dazu an?**
>
> 55 Jede Rolle und jede Position im Stück hat unter gewissen Bedingungen Recht oder bekommt durch Worte oder Handlungen Unrecht. Es lohnt sich, so widersprüchlich zu untersuchen, unsere Welt ist so.
>
> ■ **Warum sollte ein Schauspieler generell Shakespeare spielen und was bringt dies für die Arbeit an der Schule?**
>
> 60 Shakespeare ist die größte Herausforderung für Regie und Spieler. Auf leerer Bühne, bei Tageslicht, nach drei Seiten, in Interaktion mit dem Publikum spielen. Aus dem Text die Wortkulisse, das Klima, die Requisiten, die Handlungen, die Situationen zu analysieren und dann in dreigeteilter Aufmerksamkeit (zu sich, zum Partner, zum Publikum) zu spielen.
>
> 65 Das Verblüffende ist, Shakespeare hat aus irgendeinem Grund gewusst, was wir Menschen so in unserem Leben an Konflikten, Höhen und Tiefen erleben, das macht vielleicht neugierig auf seine Stücke.
> Sam Wanamaker sagte: *Don't say the words, act the words.* Im Tun, im Spielen entdeckst du intuitiv entweder emotional oder intellektuell, was du vorher nicht von
> 70 dir und anderen wusstest. Unendliches Neuland, denn jede Generation entdeckt Neues in Shakespeares Stücken.
>
> (753 Wörter)
>
> *Die Fragen an Norbert Kentrup stellten Hartmut Klose und Michael Rybicki.*

2 *Listening:* You will hear an interview with one of Shakespeare's fellow actors. The Listening Comprehension texts are on the CD-ROM in the Teacher's book. After you have listened to it once, complete the sentences.
You will hear the interview again, after which you will have a minute to finish completing the sentences. →S21

1. When Burbage and Shakespeare met they had three things in common: they _____
_____

2. Burbage's father not only _____ he was also the first to
_____

3. Before that audiences had just _____
_____

4. When the lease on The Theatre ran out they _____ ,
took it across the river and _____

5. In order to act plays, companies of actors had to _____ ,
who _____

6. The company had success both _____ and _____

7. As an actor Shakespeare was good _____ and _____

8. Under James I the troupe _____ , which meant
they were _____ and _____ more often.